Reviews

God is love – A glimpse into the untold…
"The message is beautiful and heartfelt – with explicit personal experiences. For me, it is like coming out of the deepest, darkest hole and into the light for the first time. It is not just a guide, but also a light to guide you along the way to your spiritual awakening. It is an ultimate guide when you're searching for the truth in your spiritual journey. The messages will be a constant reference for me moving forward."

Trentond

"What If Jesus Were A Coach? is one of the most unique and authentic self-help spiritual books I've read in a long time. Coach Michael Taylor cites examples and quotes from experts in a spectrum of fields and seamlessly incorporates them with a set of well-researched guidelines to help readers forge their paths to attaining spiritual enlightenment. Taylor's work touches upon the teachings of all major religions, and he makes a compelling argument on how they all guide people toward the same goal, just through different paths. Taylor's inspiring words are rooted in science, theology, and spirituality. He even cites the teachings of prominent scientists such as Albert Einstein and Nikola Tesla to drive home his message. Highly recommended."

Pikasho Deka

"What makes this book an engaging read is Taylor's experience that brings forth the idea of religious freedom. I highly recommend that you read this book if you are currently on your journey of philosophical and spiritual discovery. This book does not have all the answers, but it can shed light and somehow ease your doubts."

Vincent Dublado

WHAT IF JESUS WERE A COACH?

BY
COACH MICHAEL TAYLOR

What If Jesus Were A Coach?

Published by Creation Publishing Group LLC
www.creationpublishing.com
© 2022 Michael Taylor
ISBN # 978-1-7366369-1-6
Library of Congress Number # 2021919033

All rights reserved. No part of this book may be used, reproduced, stored in or introduced into a retrieval system, or transmitted in any form or by any means without the express written consent of the publisher.
Published and printed in the United States of America.

Contents

Reviews i
Foreword vii
Acknowledgments ix
Introduction 1
Chapter 1: My Spiritual Journey 7
Chapter 2: How Do You See God? 23
Chapter 3: Who Was Jesus? 37
Chapter 4: What Is Christianity? 49
Chapter 5: My Favorite Lessons From The Master 71
Chapter 6: Revelations 81
Chapter 7: Miracles 93
Chapter 8: Ideas Are The Currency Of The Universe 109
Chapter 9: Sin And Punishment 125
Chapter 10: Connecting To Source 141
Bio 163
Resources 165

Foreword

by Rev. Robert E. Collins,
Senior Minister | Spiritual Director
Monterey Center for Spiritual Living

Considering a career move that involved relocation, I asked myself what the long-term benefit would be for everyone involved. Feeling a sense of loneliness and excitement at the same time I remembered the writings of Michael Taylor and the empowering answers to many of my questions that seemed to jump off the page wherever I opened one of his books. I have worked with Michael on a couple of projects and always leave feeling challenged, uplifted, and prepared to face life opportunities knowing I am not alone.

Writing from his own experience, Michael presents the reader with an intimate look into his spiritual journey. He tells of his early childhood and later adult experiences with organized religion, his views of Jesus expanding from a figure to fear to Jesus as the one who is a friend and Teacher. In between these two experiences of Jesus.

Michael invited the reader to imagine what would happen if Jesus showed up at the door, engaging in a loving and supporting conversation. Not here to condemn, but to impart spiritual wisdom and encouragement.

It is important to not only read but to listen to the words Michael shares citing the paradoxes of his journey from traditional religious teachings of heaven and hell, sin and punishment, his journey through Atheism leading to his discovery of Unity and the metaphysical approach to life-affirming the inherent good in each one.

Michael speaks of the teachings of Christianity from the perspective of error thinking – being taught what to think – to the Metaphysical perspective of being taught – how to think.

Michael's insights into life are elegant and invite the reader into a place of quiet contemplation and compassion.

Acknowledgments

As a former Atheist, it is nothing short of a miracle that I'm writing a book about God. There was a time in my life when I was absolutely convinced there was no such thing. I remember how closed-minded I used to be and how I completely rejected the idea of a power greater than myself in the Universe.

Amazingly, it was my skepticism about God that led me on a journey to find the answers to the hundreds of questions I had about God. Not believing in God initially helped me search for my own individual truth about God based on science and rational thinking, which resulted in me finding "my truth" about the Divine.

It's been an amazing 30-year journey that I continue even to this day, and I am grateful for all of the lessons and miracles I've experienced along the way.

Several people have inspired, mentored, and challenged me to find my truth. And I would be remiss if I didn't acknowledge and thank them for the wisdom and guidance they've given me through their books, lectures, and programs.

First, I must always acknowledge the Divine Energy and Intelligence that created and is still creating this amazing Universe we live in. As I look at my life in retrospect, I see the Divine plan for my life and how every adversity was placed before me to support my growth and evolution. Every piece of my life's puzzle fits perfectly now, and I can clearly see exactly why I was placed on this earth at this particular time and what my divine and unique purpose for being on the planet is. Words cannot come close to expressing the pure unadulterated joy I feel daily and the only thing that comes close to being able to describe how I feel about you is to say, I love you more than love! I commit my life to being in service to you and will do all I can to express the Pure Love you are.

My all-time favorite scientist is Albert Einstein, and I must acknowledge him for being such a powerful role model for me. I love how deeply spiritual he was without claiming any religious affiliation, and his wisdom has touched me deeply while inspiring me to think critically and logically and at the same time embrace the beauty and complexity of this infinite Universe.

In 1998, I ran across a book titled; Conversations With God by Neale Donald Walsch. I had been on a spiritual journey for a few years and was trying to find my truth about God. Neale's book was instrumental in me finding my truth about God. As I read the book, I could hear God's voice whispering into my heart, "I am a God of Pure Love and I love you more than anything." I am forever grateful to Neale for sharing his wisdom. His series of books based on his conversations with God confirmed what I have always believed. The question isn't who does God talk to. The real question is, "How many of us are willing to listen?" because God speaks to all of us all of the time. I am so glad I listened and found Neale's work.

As a child, I never trusted preachers. However, after going on my own spiritual journey to find my truth, I was introduced to some amazing ministers that provided me with great insights and wisdom that helped me develop my own intimacy and connection with a power greater than myself. One of those ministers was Michael Bernard Beckwith. Michael is the founder of the Agape Spiritual Center in California. His messages of love, peace, inclusion and hope have definitely shifted my perceptions of what a minister should be like. He embodies a true spiritual leader who leads by example with an open mind and a loving heart.

When I was in my early twenty's, I read a book called Your Erroneous Zones by Dr. Wayne Dyer. In the book, he stated, "As a human being, you have within you the capacity to do anything any human being has ever done, and if it hadn't been done, you can be the first to do it." I credit Dr. Dyer with teaching me how to think and trust that still small voice within me. His teachings were definitely instrumental in my ability to overcome an assortment of adversities in my life.

Deepak Chopra is a world-renowned spiritual teacher who taught me the importance of combining science and logic with spirituality. His book, The Seven Spiritual Laws of Success, is one of my all-time favorite books, and his meditations helped me deepen my connection to Divine Intelligence. I am forever grateful for his wisdom and commitment to awakening humanity.

My mom Geneva is definitely one of my greatest teachers. From a very young age, she instilled in me a sense of infinite possibilities and optimism that is the foundation of my success. I'll never forget the greatest lesson she taught me when I was approximately ten years old, "If you want something badly enough, there is no one or no-thing that can keep you from attaining it except yourself!" Everything I am is the result of the love and guidance I received from my mom.

These are just a few of the wonderful people who have impacted my life, and for those I didn't mention here, know that I love and appreciate you for the impact you've had on my life.

Michael

Introduction

IF YOU'RE READING this book, there is a very good chance you have lots of questions about God and Jesus. I struggled with believing in God from a very early age because I had so many questions not even the minister could answer. Whenever I asked questions that no one could answer, I always received the same response, "Just pray about it!" This response fueled my skepticism about God, and eventually, it drove me to become an Atheist.

During my time as an Atheist, I was absolutely convinced that God did not exist. I didn't become an Atheist out of anger or fear. I became an Atheist because the things I was taught about God simply did not make sense to me. I could not wrap my mind around the things I was being taught through organized religion. There were so many contradictions and hypocrisies in the church that I chose to stop believing in God. Instead, I decided to try and find the answers to all of my questions through science and rational thinking. In summary, this is probably the primary reason I became an Atheist. In my mind, organized religion was irrational and illogical.

As I reflect over my life as an Atheist,, it is an absolute miracle that I'm writing this book. I remember how convinced I was that God didn't exist and there was nothing anyone could do or say that could convince me otherwise. And now, here I am, writing a book about God.

My intention in writing this book isn't to try and convince you that God exists. I intend to share the lessons I've learned along my own spiritual journey and share some answers to many of the questions I had about God that no one would or could answer.

I definitely do not claim to be an expert or religious scholar. I'm just an ordinary guy who decided to find his own "truth," and I'd like to share my truth with you. The content in this book is "my truth," not necessarily "the truth." It is up to you to find your own truth, and I hope you will find some of the answers to some questions you may have about God within the pages of this book.

I have come to know that science and spirituality are two sides of the same coin, and there is absolutely no conflict between the two. You can love science and also embrace spirituality. As a matter of fact, I do not believe you can have one without the other. I would like to share some wisdom from my all-time favorite scientist Albert Einstein to make my point. Here is something I read on his Facebook page that truly resonated with me and sums up my point about science and spirituality.

Did you know that when Einstein gave lectures at the numerous US universities he was invited to, the recurring question that students asked him was: Do you believe in God?

And he always answered:

I believe in the God of Spinoza.

The ones who hadn't read Spinoza didn't understand....

I hope this gem of history serves you as much as it does me:

Baruch de Spinoza was a Dutch philosopher considered one of the three great rationalists of 17th-century philosophy, along with René Descartes in France, and Gottfried Leibniz in Germany.

Here's some of his wisdom:

God would have said:

Stop praying and punching yourself in the chest!

What I want you to do is go out into the world and enjoy your life. I want you to enjoy, sing, have fun and enjoy everything I've made for you.

Stop going to those dark, cold temples that you built yourself and say they are my house! My house is in the mountains, in the woods, rivers, lakes, beaches. That's where I live, and there I express my love for you.

Stop blaming me for your miserable life; I never told you there was anything wrong with you or that you were a sinner, or that your sexuality was a bad thing! Sex is a gift I have given you and with which you can express your love, your ecstasy, your joy. So don't blame me for everything they made you believe.

Stop reading alleged sacred scriptures that have nothing to do with me. If you can't read me in a sunrise, in a landscape, in the look of your friends, in your son's eyes... you will find me in no book! Trust me and stop asking me. Would you tell me how to do my job?

Stop being so scared of me. I do not judge you or criticize you, nor get angry, or seek to punish you. I am pure love.

Stop asking for forgiveness, there's nothing to forgive. If I made you... I filled you with passions, limitations, pleasures, feelings, needs, inconsistencies... free will. How can I blame you if you respond to something I put in you? How can I punish you for being the way you are if I'm the one who made you? Do you think I could create a place to burn all my children who behave badly for the rest of eternity? What kind of God would do that?

Forget any kind of commandments, any kind of laws; those are wiles to manipulate you, to control you, that only create guilt in you.

Respect your peers and don't do what you don't want for yourself. All I ask is that you pay attention in your life, that your consciousness is your guide.

My beloved, this life is not a test, not a step, not a rehearsal, nor a prelude to paradise. This life is the only thing that exists here and now, and it is all you need.

I have set you absolutely free, no prizes or punishments, no sins or virtues... no one carries a marker, no one keeps a record.

You are absolutely free to create in your life heaven or hell.

I could tell you if there's anything after this life, but I won't... but I can give you a tip. Live as if there is nothing after... as if this is your only chance to enjoy, to love, to exist.

So, if there's nothing, then you will have enjoyed the opportunity I gave you. And if there is, rest assured that I won't ask if you behaved right or wrong, I'll ask. Did you like it? Did you have fun? What did you enjoy the most? What did you learn?

Stop believing in me; believing is assuming, guessing, imagining. I don't want you to believe in me... I want you to feel me in you when you kiss your beloved, when you tuck in your little girl, when you caress your dog, when you bathe in the sea.

Stop praising me, what kind of egomaniac God do you think I am?

I'm bored being praised, I'm tired of being thanked. Feeling grateful? Prove it by taking care of yourself, your health, your relationships, the world. Express your joy!... that's the way to praise me.

Stop complicating things and repeating as a parakeet what you've been taught about me.

The only thing for sure is that you are here, that you are alive, and that this world is full of wonders.

What do you need more miracles for? Why so many explanations?

Look for me outside... you won't find me. Find me inside... there I am beating within you.

Spinoza.

Just like Albert Einstein, I too, believe in the God of Spinoza. If you're open-minded and ready to find the God of Spinoza within yourself, I believe this book will serve as a great guide to support you on your spiritual journey. As you're reading this book, do not hesitate to ask yourself questions. Do not be afraid to disagree with what I'm sharing. The real challenge for you is to be willing to ask questions and then trust your inner wisdom to find your own answers. I'll be sharing insights, but it is up to you to believe or reject what I've written. As you're reading throughout this book, I'd like you to ask yourself a very simple question, "Do I really believe this?" As you ask yourself that question, listen to your heart and let it be your guide.

I have come to know that there is a power greater than yourself that permeates the Universe. You can call this power whatever you'd like, and when you learn to develop an intimacy and connection to this power, nothing will be impossible for you.

So, remember this quote as you read this book, "Who I am is God's gift to me. What I make of myself is my gift to God."

Good luck on your spiritual journey!

Michael

"Nothing binds you except your thoughts; nothing limits you except your fear; and nothing controls you except your beliefs."

— **Marianne Williamson**

CHAPTER 1
My Spiritual Journey

MY EARLIEST MEMORIES about God began when I was approximately ten years old. I remember being forced to go to church and not understanding who Jesus was. Even as a child, I struggled with the idea of Jesus because I couldn't understand why I should believe in someone or something I couldn't see. I remember asking my grandfather why I couldn't see Jesus, and his response was always the same. "You can't see him, but he is always there." This didn't answer my question about why I couldn't see him, and I believe that is when my skepticism about God began. Even as a child, I didn't believe something I couldn't see.

One thing I really hated as a child was being forced to go to church on Sundays and spending an entire day at church. I had no idea why church took so long. All I knew was I couldn't go and play with my friends on Sundays because I was always forced to go to church.

The one experience that really shaped my view of God occurred when I was forced to get baptized. I remember arguing with my grandmother about not wanting to go because I was terrified that the minister would accidentally drown me. I can still feel the terror I felt as I walked through the wading pool towards the minister with tears in my eyes. Everyone kept telling me that the holy spirit would bathe me and Jesus would come into my heart after I got baptized, but afterwards, the only thing I felt was relief. I was relieved that I did not drown and I was still alive.

I remember telling the minister that I repented my sins and I accepted Jesus as my lord and savior, but in reality, I had absolutely no idea what that meant. The only reason I said I did was that my grandmother basically threatened me with bodily harm if I didn't.

When I became a teenager, my skepticism about God increased. I have always been open-minded, curious, and unafraid to ask questions, so I began asking questions that no one could answer. For example, if God was a loving God, why in the world would he create such a thing as hell to punish people who didn't believe in him or follow his rules? Or, how in the world could a person be born a sinner when the bible said we were made in the image and after the likeness of God?

These were just two of the questions I posed to a few ministers that they could not answer. Their response was usually something like, don't question God, or just have faith that God's word is irrefutable.

During my teenage years, my mom was a single parent raising four kids. There were actually six children in our family, but my oldest brother and sister were not living with us at the time. My mom started dating, and she met this really cool guy named Al. Al was amazing. He was a brilliant and caring man who became a true father figure for me. I could talk to him about anything, and he always took the time to try and answer the unlimited number of questions I would ask.

One Sunday, my mom invited him to attend church with us. I noticed that he seemed to be a little uncomfortable with what the minister was saying during the service. His discomfort was more like disagreement. I could sense that he disagreed with a lot of things the minister had said.

After church, he and I were sitting in a park, and I asked him what he thought about the church service. He confirmed my suspicions by saying he really disagreed with most of the things the minister said. He told me it was important to think for myself and not just accept everything the minister said. He said he believed there were many paths to God, and they all led to the same place, and I should be willing to find the path that worked for me. He told me not to be afraid to ask questions and be willing to do my research and come to my own conclusions about God.

His words really comforted me and permitted me to find my truth, and from that moment on, I decided that I would take his advice and find my own path.

When I turned 18, I landed a full-time job with a building supply center and moved out and got my own apartment. Once I was out of the house, I no longer had to go to church, and that was a huge relief.

As I climbed the corporate ladder, I didn't spend much time thinking about God. As a matter of fact, it was probably the furthest thing from my mind because, at the age of 23, I was living the American Dream. I was married, bought my first house, and had two kids. By society's standards, I was successful. I had made it! But within approximately a 6 ½ year time frame, my dream turned into a nightmare as I experienced divorce, bankruptcy, foreclosure, and depression.

During this dark period in my life, I needed some help, but I didn't know which way to turn. In an attempt to alleviate some of the pain I was in, I decided I would go back to church. Even though I was skeptical and uncertain about the existence of God, I needed to do something to try and get back on my feet.

Since I was brought up Baptist, I found a Baptist church and started to attend regularly. The minister was a lot different from the minister from my childhood. He was much more positive and uplifting, and he actually inspired me. I truly enjoyed going to church for a while.

But after a couple of months, the questions from my childhood kept creeping up. I still had a lot of unanswered questions that needed to be answered, and those questions were like a splinter in my mind that I couldn't remove.

One night, I was sitting up late because there was a question that had been bugging me for my entire life. I kept asking myself this question repeatedly in my mind, and I needed the minister to answer it for me.

The following Sunday, I asked the minister if I could speak with him after the service. He agreed, and after services, we met in his office. I told him I had a question I needed to ask him, and his answer to the question would determine whether or not I would stay with his church.

He looked a little confused, but he assured me he would answer the question to the best of his ability.

I then posed this hypothetical question to him. "I want you to imagine there are two men who are born at exactly the same time under two completely different circumstances. One man is born into extreme wealth and the other is born in abject poverty. Now imagine the man who is born into poverty becomes a criminal. He robs and steals and possibly even takes someone's life. On the other hand, the person who is born into wealth is a model citizen. He feeds the hungry, shares his wealth, and by all intents and purposes, he is a good man.

Now imagine they die at exactly the same time, and they both wind up at the entrance to heaven. Standing at the gate is God Almighty, and he is standing behind a podium looking at his book of life. God tells the man born in poverty to step forward and begins reviewing the man's life in his book of life. He then looks at the man and says, "You have really done some awful things. But I am a God of love and forgiveness, and I have one simple question to ask. Do you or did you accept my son Jesus Christ as your Lord and savior?"

The man looks up at God and says, "God, I have made a lot of mistakes in my life, and I am truly sorry for them. I repent of my sins, and I accept your son as my lord and savior."

God smiles at the man and allows him to enter into heaven.

Next, he calls up the man who was born into wealth. He begins reviewing his life, and a large smile comes across his face. He looks at the man and says, "You have been a wonderful and loving human being. You epitomized me in every way possible. Your actions have been admirable, and now all I need to hear from you is that you accepted my son as your lord and savior, and then I can welcome you into heaven."

The man looks up at God with some trepidation and then he says, "Well, God, there is a small problem. I can't accept your son as lord and savior because, first of all, I've never even believed that you even existed."

So God looks at the man and then tells him he will have to spend an eternity in hell, and he sends the man off to hang out with Satan."

So, after sharing this hypothetical story, I asked the minister if that was how his God works. Without hesitation, he looked me straight in the eye and said yes, that is what the bible teaches, and that is what he believed.

At that moment, years of anger and frustration surfaced, and I looked at the minister and respectfully asked him, "Are you out of your mind? That is the most irrational belief I've ever heard. How in the world can you believe that nonsense? I tell you what, I am willing to risk eternal damnation because, in my heart of hearts, there is no way that a loving God would ever do such a thing. I sincerely respect your beliefs, but after this conversation, I am very clear on what I believe. There really is no such thing as God, so from this moment on, I am leaving your church and letting go of the idea of this fictitious being the world has created."

In that very moment, I became an Atheist. I walked away from that church and from God, and I actually felt a deep sense of relief and freedom by making that decision.

After that conversation, I began researching Atheism. I became extremely comfortable with my newfound beliefs and started focusing my attention on science and personal growth. I then concluded that science and rational thinking was all I needed in my life. As an Atheist, I didn't go around condemning or being judgmental about other people's beliefs. As a matter of fact, I did just the opposite. I was so comfortable with my beliefs I had no need to argue or defend them. Therefore I was very comfortable with opposing views about God because I knew exactly what I believed and allowed others to believe what they believed without judgment.

After a few years of being an Atheist, I became deeply involved with personal development and healing my childhood wounds. As I continued my healing process, my life got better, and I became happier, but something was still missing that I couldn't quite put my finger on. During my healing journey, I began a practice of meditation in an effort to quiet my mind and feel more peaceful. My meditation practice led me to Buddhist teachings that began to change my mind about the possibility of God existing. During one of my meditations, I had a profound revelation. I realized I had gone about it the wrong way. Rather than completely reject the idea of God, why not research God and come to my own conclusions?

This question led me to begin my search for the truth that would set me free. I started by researching the bible and gaining a better understanding of who wrote it and how it came to be. I was intrigued by how many different versions of Christianity there were, and I took a lot of time studying exactly what Jesus said and how to use what he said to improve my life.

After studying Christianity, I decided to research other religions. I spent a lot of time with Buddhist monks because of my meditation practice, and Buddhism was actually the first spiritual practice in which I felt something spiritual. What I love about Buddhism is it isn't really a religion. It is a practice of mindfulness, which is designed to help you connect with your Buddha-nature. Unlike Christianity, it doesn't preach that you have to do anything out of duty and obligation. There is no guilt or condemnation, and you aren't seen as a sinner that has to earn your way back into the good graces of God. Even today, I love spending time in Buddhist temples in quiet contemplation.

I also learned a lot of spiritual truths through the Bhagavad Gita and the Vedas and Upanishads from the Hindu religion. Hindus believe in multiple Gods (which I find fascinating), and there is a sacredness about Hindu temples that I really love.

I went to a Jewish synagogue, learned about the Kabbalah, and had one of the deepest and thought-provoking conversations about life with a Jewish Rabbi. Like me, he was an intriguing fellow who shared a deep love for science, and he was able to incorporate science into his religion. I really enjoyed our talk and came away from it with a deep respect for the Jewish religion.

I was also deeply intrigued by a conversation I had with a man at a Muslim Mosque. I learned that Muslims actually believed in Jesus; they simply didn't believe he was the Messiah or Divine Son of God. They acknowledge his divinity and miracles and even talk about him in their Holy Book, the Quran.

After several years on my spiritual journey, I had a change of heart and started to believe in God. Even though I had spent a lot of time researching religions and concluded that all religions actually teach the same thing as Al had said, I was still mystified by the story of Jesus and wanted to learn more about his life. I then received a miracle that would answer every question I had about Jesus, and it would ultimately become the foundation of my spiritual beliefs.

I attended a personal development workshop called LifeSpring. During the workshop, I had a conversation about God with one of the other participants. She asked me if I had ever heard of a church called Unity, and I told her no. She then told me that I would love it because it was a positive approach to Christianity, and she said I was the most positive person she ever met, and she knew I would fit right in. She even mentioned they were so positive that sometimes she didn't go because she was actually uncomfortable with so much positivity.

A part of me was a little hesitant, but since I wanted to learn more about Jesus's life, I told her I would eventually check it out.

Here is where the miracle happened.

The very next day, I was at home sitting at my kitchen table, looking through a phone book for something. All of a sudden, my phone rang, so I got up to answer it. When I got up, I accidentally knocked the phone book onto the floor. After I completed my call, I picked up the phone book, and when I laid it on the table and looked inside, there was an advertisement for Unity Church. I smiled because I immediately recognized the synchronicity and jotted down the phone number to give them a call.

It turned out the church was only a few minutes away from where I lived, so I knew I was supposed to go. I decided to drive by even though they were closed just to check it out. As I looked through the window of their bookstore, I was pleasantly surprised to see books from some of my favorite authors regarding personal growth and spirituality. Now I was really excited and couldn't wait until Sunday.

When Sunday came around, I parked out front and decided to see what type of people would be going in. I knew there would probably not be many black people attending because this was definitely not a traditional church setting. I decided to go in, and I experienced another miracle.

There are some events in our lives that change the trajectory we are on forever. Some people would call them transcendent experiences, while others might use the word divine. I'm not sure exactly what to call it, but as soon as I stepped into the church, something in me shifted. A part of me screamed with joy and delight as if knowing I had found my home. I could never fully explain it in words, but the closest I can come to describing it is by saying I was bathed by a holy spirit. It was a palpable feeling of being touched by something divine. My soul lit up like a Christmas tree inside.

Once I walked in, my suspicions were confirmed. I was the only black person in the church, but it definitely didn't bother me because I was surrounded by nothing but love. I could feel the unconditional non-judgmental feeling of acceptance, and it felt wonderful.

The first thing the minister said was, "It's time to begin our service with a meditation." What? Do they meditate in a Christian church? Is this real? I remember telling one of my Christian friends that I had begun meditating, and she said meditation was trafficking with the devil. And now, there I was in a Christian church, meditating. Had I died and gone to heaven? It sure felt that way.

After the meditation, the minister gave a loving and inspiring sermon that opened my heart and filled me with the divine love of God. It was absolutely beautiful.

After the service, I was greeted and acknowledged for coming, and of course, they extended an invitation for me to join their church. Although I knew I would eventually be joining the church, I declined their invitation so I could learn more about it. The experience was so new and different from what I was accustomed to. Thus, I wanted to make sure I wasn't being pulled into some type of cult or something.

So I grabbed some of their material and went home to learn more. During my research, I learned that Unity began in 1889 with Charles and Myrtle Fillmore. It is a nondenominational New Thought church that teaches a metaphysical interpretation of the bible that encourages its congregants to recognize that every human being has a spark of divinity within them, and Jesus came to teach you how to access that spark.

Although I was impressed with what I learned about the church, it wasn't the material that convinced me to want to join. It was that feeling I received the moment I walked in, and it was my own inner wisdom that was guiding me to join.

During that time in my life, I was experiencing a lot of adversities and difficulties, and I ended up having to move away from my home in Houston. I actually moved away to live with my brother because I didn't have a job and I had run out of money.

I moved to Austin, and the first thing I did was find a Unity church. I started attending services regularly, and I committed myself to their teachings. One of their teachings is that there is but one presence and one power in the Universe, God the good omnipotent. Therefore, if I am experiencing any adversity or challenge, it isn't that I'm being punished; I'm simply being redirected to something better. So despite my financial situation, I accepted this truth and held firm to the belief that I was being guided to something bigger and better in my life.

Although it was difficult, I held firm to this belief for a couple of years before my life actually started getting better. But those challenges only deepened my faith, and ultimately, things started turning around, and I was able to get back on my feet and move back to Houston.

Once there, I immediately found another Unity church. After the years of following their principles, I had developed my faith from just believing in God to knowing there was God. With this newfound faith, I decided it was time to fully commit to the Unity teachings by becoming a member.

Nevertheless, a part of me still had some negative residual effects from joining the Baptist church. I then decided that I would go and speak to the minister before I joined just to remove any doubt that I was doing the right thing.

When I met with the minister, I told him the story about why I had left the Baptist church. I also told him that I really didn't trust preachers, but my beliefs had definitely changed since joining Unity. He then said something that would put my mind at ease and confirm I was making the right decision. He smiled at me and said, "The most important thing for you to understand is I am no closer to God than you are.

You have the same access to God that I have. My job is to simply help you deepen your connection to God because that is where your inner peace and power will come from. Therefore, your relationship isn't with me. Your relationship is direct with God." There was a calmness and sincerity in his words that truly comforted me. Unlike the experience I had with the Baptist minister, I had a deep sense of connection and sincerity with this Unity minister. A part of me knew I had found my church home, and my soul was comforted by my decision to join.

From that point on, I joined the church and I became truly committed to the Unity teachings. I took several courses and attended lectures to learn all I could about the Universal principles they taught. I even taught Sunday school to teenagers and even considered becoming a Unity minister but then decided against it because I concluded that I didn't have to be a minister to have a ministry. I then began my ministry by writing books and becoming a speaker who shares the wisdom and lessons I've learned on my own spiritual journey with others. I have now created my version of an extraordinary life, and I am happier now than I've ever been in my life. Has it been easy? Of course not! Was it all worth it? Absolutely, unequivocally, yes!

As I reflect over the past 25 years or so of my spiritual journey, I'm in awe of the grace and love of God. As I look back, I can see how every adversity, no matter how difficult or painful, brought me a gift and a lesson that was for my highest good. If I had to do my life all over again, I wouldn't change a thing because I now see the perfection in all of it. If I had changed any part of it, I wouldn't be the man I am today.

At the beginning of this book, I mentioned that my intention wasn't to try and convince you that God existed. However, I would like to share a couple of truths that have allowed me to develop an intimacy and connection with a power greater than myself that allows me to know beyond a shadow of a doubt that God is real. I'm not asking you to believe what I say, but I am asking you to simply contemplate these ideas and see if they resonate with you.

First of all, you need to find your own truth about God. Most people simply accept what has been passed on to them without truly asking themselves what they really believe. So my suggestion for you is to honestly ask yourself what you believe and why you believe it. Be willing and open to the idea that what you may have believed in the past isn't true. Be willing to be wrong about God so ultimately you'll be right about God. In other words, find what's true for you. To do this, you will have to challenge some deeply held beliefs but rest assured when you authentically find your truth, it will be worth any discomfort you may have to go through.

Next, always remember there are many paths to God, and just because someone is on a different path than you are doesn't mean they are the ones who are lost. Find your truth and allow others to find theirs. I can assure you if you find your authentic truth, it will not matter what other people believe, and you will not feel the need to try and convince others that your truth is the truth. Find your truth!

Last but definitely not least, develop intimacy and connection to a power greater than yourself. Remember, the name isn't important, but nurturing and creating the connection is. My suggestion is to develop a spiritual practice that keeps you connected to this power. Let me recommend that meditation practice is one of the best ways to create and maintain that connection.

In closing, my hope is that you have an opportunity to experience the unconditional love of a loving Creator. It is a feeling that is so deep you could never put it into words. It is like feeling the unconditional love of a child or being kissed by the beauty of a sunrise or sunset. It is joy, it is passion, it is reverence and love all rolled up into one thing. It is God, and yet that word doesn't come close to expressing what it is. Skip the word and go for the feeling. Ultimately, it's even more than a feeling; it's the reality of the whole world, and I hope you get to feel it!

I want to share another miracle I experienced which confirmed the presence of God in my life. One day, I came home from church after a powerful message. I didn't have a car at the time, and I would ride my bike to church, which was approximately an hour away. While I was lying on my floor in my run-down efficiency apartment with no furnishings except an air mattress, I started to thank God for the things that I did have. I had just purchased a copy of BeBe and Cece Winans gospel tape "Different Lifestyles," and I had a portable cassette player with headphones. As I lay on my air-mattress and listened to the tape, I started listening to a song titled "Searching for Love."

As I listened to the words, they were singing about searching for love, and he asked the question, "Has anyone found it?" He goes on to say that he found it, and it's more than just a feeling. It's the reality of the whole world. He continued, "Love in the form of a babe that was born to reveal that love he was talking about." As I lay there listening to the song, I started looking back over the last few years of my life. I remembered my nice home and family, my credit cards, and my nice secure job. Then I looked around at the bare walls of my apartment and looked at my bicycle, which was my only form of transportation. I had a total of sixteen dollars to my name and was over twenty thousand dollars in debt.

I continued to listen to the words, and suddenly, something started happening in my gut. I kept listening to the words of the song and started thinking about my three-year search for God. I began visualizing the message at church, and I kept going back to where I used to be. Suddenly, that feeling that started in my gut reached my chest, and then it felt as if my heart exploded with joy. And I realized I had found the love he was singing about. I realized that even though I didn't have all the material things that I had several years ago, I had never been happier in my life. I was experiencing life's ultimate paradox; to have absolutely nothing yet have absolutely everything simultaneously. I had found God and was feeling it move through me. I cannot express the love and joy that came from within. I lay there on that mattress and cried for three hours straight. I kept listening to that song repeatedly, and it was as if God was speaking directly to me. For the first time, I was complete. Although it had taken me a few years, I had found exactly what I was looking for, and I had finally found the missing link in my life. I had confirmation that God is real. My life hasn't been the same since. But now I don't just believe in God, I know God. There is a huge distinction between the two.

I realize that everyone must ultimately make their own choice about God, and I would never say that what I believe is the only way. I would like to suggest that if you have experienced emptiness and pain in your life, creating a connection with a power greater than yourself is definitely a solution.

The one thing I always hated about religion was the fact that people would try to force you to believe what they believed. This is probably why so many people shy away from religion. But I want to suggest that there is a huge distinction to be made between religion and spirituality.

I define spirituality as, "The moment-to-moment recognition and acknowledgment of my connection to something greater than myself," which means recognizing God as my source but understanding I am completely responsible for my actions. Unity teaches me that Christianity is a way of life, and if I choose to accept this way of life, then my actions have to be consistent with my beliefs. Instead of being labeled a "Christian," I simply need to follow the teachings of Jesus and my life works.

Spirituality, for me, means that every day is an opportunity for me to experience the joy of being alive. Creating an attitude of gratitude that says "Thanks, God" for this wonderful gift called "life." Knowing that God has a purpose for me and that my life is a miracle when I choose to accept that purpose.

I hope my spiritual journey has provided you with some fuel for contemplation. In the following chapters, I'm going to share some ideas that I believe will answer many questions you may have about God and about Jesus. Once again, I'm sharing "my truths", and I hope that you will gain some insights that will support you in developing a deeper connection with a power greater than yourself. I choose to call this power Divine Intelligence, and you get to call it whatever you'd like.

With that being said, I'll close this chapter with this:

I believe that God is like Coke. It's The Real Thing! Some people drink Coke out of a can, some drink it out of a bottle, some people drink it out of chilled glasses, and some people drink it out of plastic containers. Some people consume large amounts, and others drink small amounts. But ultimately, the container that it's in really doesn't matter. The only thing that matters is quenching your thirst with the Coke.

God is the spiritual "Thirst Quencher!" Like Coke, it can be held in different containers, but ultimately, the container really doesn't matter. What does matter is if you are getting your spiritual thirst quenched. Basically, six containers hold The Real Thing, Christianity, Judaism, Hinduism, Confucianism, Islam, and Buddhism. Then you have the straws that are used to drink out of the container. Example: Christianity is the container and Methodist, Catholic, Protestant, and Baptist are the straws. But as I've mentioned, they all contain God. Of course, most religions think that their container is the right container, but that is simply their belief.

According to The New International Student Bible, (1Corinthians 12:12) states, "The body is a unit, though it is made up of many parts; and though its parts are many, they form one body. So, it is with Christ. For we were all baptized by one Spirit into one body -whether Jews or Greeks, slaves or free, and we were all given the one Spirit to drink."

I believe that this spirit is God.

My question to you is, "Are you quenching your spiritual thirst?

"I looked for God and found only myself, and then I looked for myself, and found only God"

- **Rumi**

CHAPTER 2
How Do You See God?

Growing up as a child, I remember the picture of Jesus hanging up in my grandparents' home. It was the familiar picture of the white Jesus with a light emanating from his heart, symbolizing his love for humanity. I also remember the Jesus nailed on the cross wall hanging sculpture which also hung on their walls. Even as a child, I didn't understand why Jesus was white, and why did he hate black people so much?

You see, my grandparents were extremely religious even though they never went to church. As I mentioned in the previous chapter, they forced me to go to church, yet they never attended. This definitely caused some major conflicts in my mind because even though they talked a lot about Jesus, their actions did not reflect Jesus' teachings. My grandmother was a raging alcoholic who physically and verbally abused me. How could I follow Jesus when the grownup responsible for raising me was such a terrible person?

On the other hand, my grandfather was a quiet gentleman who was deeply religious and filled with wisdom. Even though he only had an eighth-grade education, he was one of the smartest men I've ever known. Some of my fondest memories from childhood were having conversations with him just about anything. We would sit outside in the yard amongst a myriad of farm animals, and he would share stories about a wide variety of topics, including life. Even though I was just a kid, he talked to me as though I was much older, and he challenged me to always think about things very deeply.

One day, I asked him why God was so angry at black people. This was during the civil rights movement as I watched news stories of black people being attacked by dogs, sprayed with fire hoses, and being beaten by cops. My young ten-year-old mind couldn't understand why black people were maltreated. So in my mind, I concluded that black people must have done something really bad since Jesus didn't step in and stop the abuse black people were enduring.

When I asked the question, he picked up on the sadness and fear in my voice, and he lifted me and placed me on his knee. He then told me that God wasn't angry at black people. He said that God had a perfect plan, and even though we may not fully understand it, God's plan was perfect. But how could God's plan be so perfect while black people were being so mistreated? He told me not to worry and to trust the divine plan of God.

As a ten-year-old, I couldn't fully understand what he meant. I tried to rationalize how God's plan was perfect, but I just couldn't see it. In retrospect, and as an adult now, I can definitely understand the perfection of the plan he was talking about. Still, it has taken me years of deep self-introspection and research to fully grasp the implications of what my grandfather told me.

I'm reminded of a quote by Albert Einstein that said, "If you can't explain your subject to an eighth-grader, you don't fully understand your topic." With that being said, I'd like to share how I now see God and how I came to my understanding.

First of all, I think most people see God as this anthropomorphic being that resides up in heaven somewhere. Since most people in the West are Christians, they have this common view that God is some old guy in the clouds who is taking notes of their lives and waiting for them to "sin" so he can banish them to eternal damnation in a fiery hell. This is one of the greatest erroneous filled teachings of most organized western religions. The error is thinking and believing that God is a human being just like us. Since God is just like us, he must have human emotions and needs, and therefore organized religions have built an entire theology based on the idea that God acts like a human. Why else would he create the ten commandments? Why else would we have to prove our love for him so he wouldn't punish us? Does it make sense to you that an omniscient and omnipresent God would get angry at you for making mistakes? Does it make sense to you that God is a jealous God? These things do not make sense to me, which is why I've always had an issue with organized religion.

The reason most people see God as a human being can be traced to Genesis 1:27, where it says, "So God created man in his own image, in the image of God he created him; male and female he created them." This verse has been misinterpreted, and most religions have concluded that this passage implies that God looks like a human being. But if you read John 4:24, it should clarify who and what God is. It says, "God is spirit, and his worshipers must worship in the Spirit and in truth."

As it says, "God is spirit," and since we were made in the image and after the likeness of God, that means we are spirit also.

According to Dr. Wayne Dyer (author and spiritual teacher), we are not human beings having a spiritual experience, we are spiritual beings having a human experience. If you can embrace this idea, rest assured this book will make a lot more sense.

Since most people see Jesus as the personification of God in human form, they have accepted this erroneous belief that God must think and act just like a human being. This is the origin of most conflicts in the world. Believing that God is a "who" instead of a "what." It is my belief that God is the Divine Intelligence that created and is still creating this amazing Universe we live in. Therefore, I see God as more of a "what" than a "who." Seeing God this way answers another question I had as a child. Where was God before the Universe began?

To answer that question, let's begin by listening to two of the most brilliant men and greatest minds the world has ever seen.

Albert Einstein once said, "Everything is energy, that's just the way that it is. Match the frequency of the reality you want to create and there is no way you can't create that reality. It can be no other way. This isn't philosophy, this is physics."

Nikola Tesla said, "If you want to understand the Universe, you must think in terms of energy, frequency, and vibration."

Both of these brilliant minds point to a scientific fact. Everything is energy!

So, where did this energy come from? This is the million-dollar question!

To answer it, you have three options.

Option 1. It was a random act that just happened.

Option 2. Something caused it to happen.

Option 3. You do not know where it came from.

Option number one is based on science. Science says there was a Big Bang that occurred randomly and the Universe is the result of a chemical reaction that evolved into our current Universe.

Option number two is based on a belief that a Creator caused the Universe to take form. Every religion is based on this option.

Option number three is, "I really do not know!"

So which option best describes what you believe, Option #1, Option #2, or Option #3?

To help you choose which option you believe, let's go back several thousand years. Try to imagine what it must have been like to be a caveman. During that time, your primary responsibility was to provide food and shelter for you and your family and protect yourself and your family from being eaten alive by dinosaurs. For the most part, it was a pretty simple life. You didn't have language, but you learned to communicate with pictures and sounds. As cave dwellers evolved, they developed language and learned to make weapons and basic tools for their survival. As they continued to evolve, they realized certain things that they didn't understand or have control over, so they came up with stories and ideas to try and make sense of natural phenomena. For example, if lightning strikes, they had no idea where the lightning came from, so they created stories to explain where it originated from.

They then came up with the idea that there was some sort of powerful force in the sky that was shooting lightning bolts at them. If they contracted a disease, they created stories that said the gods up in the sky were angry and were punishing them for one reason or another. So, it was man's lack of understanding of the physical world around them that caused them to come up with explanations of things they didn't understand. Therefore, these stories became religions.

As these stories were passed down from generation to generation, human beings were still evolving. Some significantly evolved beings began teaching that there was a Creator of all things, and they provided some new stories about how this Creator operated. These evolved beings laid the groundwork for all religions, and their teachings spread across the globe.

The problem as I see it was each of these evolved beings shared a message of oneness with the Creator. However, each evolved being had their own unique interpretation of what the Creator was expecting from human beings, and they shared their "truth" with the masses, and then the masses started sharing those truths with others. Unfortunately, many of the evolved being's messages got lost in translation and were misinterpreted and even completely changed. Yet, the masses concluded that their evolved being was the chosen evolved being, and if you didn't follow their evolved being's way of worshipping God, you could not be a part of their evolved being's tribe. So, each tribe believed their evolved being was teaching the "right" way to connect with God, and the other evolved beings were teaching the "wrong" way of connecting with God.

Therefore, religion is a belief in a story of an evolved being that came to teach human beings how to connect to the Creator. The downside of religion is that they promote exclusivity. If you do not believe in their teachings, you are seen as different and separate from that particular group. In other words, if you do not believe in what they believe, you cannot be a part of their tribe. This is the core essence of religion.

On the other hand, you have spirituality. Spirituality suggests that several evolved beings have walked the earth, and each one shared the same message. Their primary message is that there is a Divine

Creator of the Universe, and every human being has equal access to this Creator. Being spiritual but not religious means recognizing that all religions originate from the same source and lead to the same place. Therefore, you accept that some people may believe in a different God other than yours, but that doesn't mean they can't be a part of your tribe. Spirituality is all-inclusive and welcomes all human beings into one Universal tribe.

There was a time when I believed in option #1. As I mentioned earlier, I concluded there was no such thing as God, and I held firm to the belief that science had the answer to everything, and if it couldn't be proved by science, it simply wasn't real. But then I made a paradigm shift. I changed my rigid way of thinking by researching the different religions and coming to my own conclusions and beliefs about God.

To provide you with some fuel for contemplation, I'd like to share some things I've learned that confirm for me that science and spirituality actually go together. I realize that some people may not believe this, but I will assume you are open-minded enough to believe what I am about to share since you're still reading.

Let's go back to the quote, "everything is energy." There is a scientific process called reductionism, which means you can take anything and reduce it down to its smallest component to know exactly what it is made of. There was a time when scientists thought the smallest particle of matter was the atom, so they concluded that the atom was the building block of all matter. As science evolved and technology increased, they realized the atom wasn't the smallest particle of matter. When they broke down everything into its smallest component, they realized that everything was actually composed of energy. In other words, nothing is actually solid. It's energy vibrating at different speeds, and as this energy slows down, it becomes solid matter. Dr. Joe Dispenza explained it this way, "If you stripped an atom down to its raw essentials, all that exists is energy and information, but the atom is not without design. Even at that quantum level, there exists a structure and orderliness, so there must be some intelligence or force that is unifying and ordering them."

So, what is this intelligence or force, and where did it come from?

Once again, this is the million-dollar question. Did this energy and intelligence randomly appear or did "something" cause it to appear?

As a result of my own research, I have come to some conclusions on my own that I would like to share with you. To fully grasp what I'm about to share, it may require you to create a new paradigm on what you believe about how the Universe began.

I'd like you to try to imagine complete darkness and emptiness. Put another way, try to imagine complete nothingness. In this nothingness, nothing exists. There is no light or darkness, or even time. It is pure nothingness. Can you imagine it? Now try to imagine that all of a sudden, something came from nothing. If you believe in science, the instant that something came from nothing was called the Big Bang. If you're religious, it was in that moment that God said, "Let there be light." Either way, the point here is at first, there was nothing, and then there was something. If you choose to see this event from a scientific perspective, how would you explain that? If there was absolute nothingness and then something came from nothing, that means the nothingness was actually something because it would be impossible for something to come from nothing. Are you still with me here? Think deeply about that. How could something come from nothing? I would like to propose that the nothingness is actually something, and that something could be called Pure Consciousness, Divine Intelligence. You could even call it Love, which is the highest vibration in the Universe. If you're religious, you can call it God. As I see it, it is the Source of all things. Everything in the Universe arises from this Divine Intelligence. The instant something came from nothing, an energy was released and there is an intelligence that drives this energy. The intelligence that drives this energy is called evolution. Evolution is the process through which Divine Intelligence evolves to deeper and deeper levels of complexity and this is an ongoing process that will continue throughout eternity.

This energy is within you, and true spirituality is developing an intimacy with and connection to this energy. You do not have to be religious to connect to this energy. Even if you do not believe in this energy, it is still there. Each religion is supposed to help you recognize this energy within you. Unfortunately, most religions get caught up in religious dogma and doctrine and fail to teach you the truth of accessing this energy.

This answers my question of where was God before the Universe began? God was everywhere because God is everything. If God were a human being, where would he/she have been before the Universe began? Hmmm?

I do not believe we can fully grasp exactly what God is in our limited human minds. By choosing to see God as Love, Divine Intelligence or Pure Consciousness, it allows us to grasp the idea of God and yet it doesn't fully explain what God truly is. It's like trying to imagine how long eternity is. Eternity is forever. It never stops. So is God; it is everything and nothing at the same time. It doesn't come to an end.

Now that I've shared how I see God, I'd like to share another thing I've learned about God and the Holy Trinity. Have you ever had someone try to explain the Holy Trinity to you? The Trinity states that there is The Father, The Son, and The Holy Spirit, yet they are all supposed to be the same thing. How is that possible? This is incredibly confusing, and I definitely had difficulty understanding it based on traditional Christianity, so I would like to share my perception of the Holy Trinity.

To start, let's take a look at Genesis Chapter 1 verse 26. "Then God said, "Let us make man in our image, in our likeness, and let them rule over the fish of the sea and the birds of the air, over the livestock, over all the earth and over all the creatures that move along the ground."

Let me preface this explanation with a little caveat. I do not believe in the literal interpretation of the bible. I believe in the metaphysical interpretation. This means the stories in the bible are metaphorical, allegorical, and not written to be taken literally but to be understood spiritually and metaphorically. Therefore, each story provides us with an opportunity to learn something about ourselves to help us grow into the best version of ourselves.

One question I could never get a minister to answer was based on that quote from Genesis 1:26. Why did God say, "Let "us" make man in "our" image?" Who was he referring to when he said that? Why didn't he say let me make man in my image?

I've never had anyone explain this to me, so I'm certain someone reading this has the same question, so now I'd like to share my answer.

Let's go back to the beginning. Remember when I said there was nothing, and then all of a sudden, there was something? The nothingness was God or Pure Consciousness. The instant something came from nothing, something was "born." That something which was born could be referred to as an energy. Since the bible was written by men from a patriarchal point of view, we use the term "Father," but in reality, "Mother" would have been more appropriate since men do not give birth, but for the sake of this discussion, we will leave that alone. So, the "Father," which is God or Divine Intelligence, gave birth to an energy which we will call its son. If you practice Christianity, you would call this son Christ. If you follow the Tao, you would call this son Chi, and if you're Native American, you would call this son Catori. Regardless of what you call it, it is an energy that originated from the Father or Creator. So now you have the father and the son, but what about the Holy Spirit? The Holy Spirit is the individual expression of the son.

Think of it this way. There is a spark of divinity in every human being. You have it, I have it, everyone has it. This spark, this energy, is divine, and it is your birthright. This spark, which was birthed by the Father and expressed by the son, needed a way to be expressed, so God created man/woman to be the divine expression of itself.

Here is a simple story to illustrate what I mean.

Once upon a time, God was sitting up in heaven looking down at the earth at human beings with a few of his angels when he became overwhelmed with pride. "Human beings are without question my greatest creations. I want to give them something that I didn't give to any other creatures on earth; I want to give them a part of me. But I don't want to just give it to them; I want them to earn it so they will truly appreciate this divine gift. So, I need to figure out a place to put it where they will have to put forth some effort to find it. Where do you think I should put it?

One of the angels spoke up and said, "I know where you can put it. Why not put it on top of the tallest mountain? God thought about it for a moment, and then he said, "I don't think that's a good idea. Human beings will easily climb the highest mountain and find this gift."

Then another angel spoke up, "I know where to hide it. Why not put it at the bottom of the ocean? Surely it would þe difficult for man to find it there."

Once again, God thought about it and said, "I don't think so. Human beings are naturally curious, and I don't think they would have any problems finding it at the bottom of the ocean."

Then another angel spoke up, "Why not place it amongst the stars? Surely the human beings would find it difficult finding it among the stars."

God pondered the idea for a moment and responded the same way. "Human beings are ingenious and adventurous. I don't think it would be hard for them to find it among the stars.

Then another angel walked up to God and said, "I know the perfect place for you to hide it. I am certain it would be the last place human beings would ever look. Why not put your divine spark inside of them?"

All of a sudden, a huge smile came across God's face. "That is brilliant! What a great idea. I agree with you totally, so I will place my divine spark inside of every human being, and it will be up to them to find it."

This story serves as a perfect metaphor for what the Holy Spirit is. It is a divine spark of God which gives us access to God in our own unique individual way, and it is our responsibility to find it. No one can find it for us.

One of my favorite quotes is, "If you don't go within, you will always go without." Therefore, if you are unwilling to look within your own heart and mind, you will never find God. Most religions have promoted the idea that God is somewhere outside of you, but the truth is, God has always been inside of you.

Going back to the story I shared about God looking down on earth at human beings and being proud of his creations, God came up with the perfect plan to find a way to express itself on earth. In Genesis 1:27, it says, "So God created man in his own image, in the image of God he created him; male and female he created them." Verse 28 says, "God blessed them and said to them: Be fruitful and multiply; fill the earth and subdue it. Rule over the fish of the sea and the birds of the air and over every living creature that moves on the ground."

The way I interpret those two verses is, God made it clear that human beings were its greatest creation. They were given a divine part of God, and therefore, they had dominion over all other creations. Looking at it from a metaphysical perspective, human beings are divine individual expressions of God.

Think of it this way.

Take a moment and think about the ocean. If you stand on a beach and look towards the horizon, it looks infinite, it looks beautiful, it looks powerful, and it looks majestic. Now imagine that you have a jar, and you walk to the ocean and scoop up a jar of ocean. The jar of ocean has the exact same qualities, characteristics, and attributes of the ocean. It is, in fact, the ocean. There is no difference. But can the jar of ocean be the ocean in its totality? No! It is an individual expression of the ocean, but it cannot be the entire ocean. And yet, there is absolutely no difference.

This is another way to see God. God is the ocean, and you are an individual expression of God. You have all of the same qualities, characteristics, and attributes of God, but you could never be God in its totality.

Put another way, you are a divine personality in the mind of God. As personalities in the mind of God, God communicates with us through divine ideas. Ideas are the currency of the Universe, and when you learn to quiet the noise of your mind and move into the silence of your heart, then you will hear the voice of your soul, which are the divine ideas that come directly from God. I'll be sharing more about this in the next chapter.

I'd like to close this chapter with a very important question. As a matter of fact, it's possibly the most important question you've ever been asked. So when I ask the question, I want you to take a moment and truly think about it before you answer. Spend some time in deep contemplation, and then answer the question as honestly as you can. Try not to allow other people's opinions or what you have been taught to believe to influence your answer. Listen to your own heart and mind and answer truthfully. No one needs to know your answer except you.

Are you ready?

What are your beliefs about God?

Notice I didn't ask you if you believe in God; I asked what your beliefs about God are. For some people, they may not believe God exists. For other people, they may have a very strong belief in God. Some may believe in an anthropomorphic god sitting in heaven, taking notes of their lives and waiting for them to die to see if they can get into heaven. Others may believe in a God of love who loves them unconditionally and accepts them with open, loving arms and showers them with grace.

So if you truly want to know what type of God you believe in, let me suggest you simply take a deep look at your life right now, and you will find your answer. Always remember, your belief about a thing creates your experience of that thing. If you believe in an angry, judgmental God to whom you have to repent of your sins to try and get into heaven, chances are your life is filled with fear and anxiety. On the other hand, if you believe in a God of love, your life could be filled with joy, inner peace, and happiness.

But ultimately, your beliefs about God will always create your experience of God, so it's important to be really clear about what you believe. I am convinced most people really do not know what they believe about God. They may know what they were taught to believe about God through their families and cultures, but they have never really questioned or challenged those beliefs. They have simply accepted beliefs that may have been passed down for generations, and they are absolutely convinced that their beliefs are the "right" beliefs and anyone who doesn't believe what they believe is "wrong."

It is now up to you to decide how you see God. I hope this chapter has provided you with some fuel for contemplation and some insights that will support you in creating an intimate connection to a power greater than yourself.

Rest assured, when you do, your life will become miraculous!

"So I say to you, **Ask and it will be given to you**; search, and you will find; knock, and the door will be opened for you. Do not be anxious about tomorrow, for tomorrow will be anxious for itself. Let the day's own trouble be sufficient for the day. And know that I am with you always; yes, to the end of time."

- **Jesus**

CHAPTER 3
Who Was Jesus?

I'D LIKE YOU to take a moment and see what thoughts and feelings come up for you when I mention the word, Jesus? Are the thoughts and feelings positive, or are they negative? For most of my young life, whenever I heard the word Jesus, it would bring up some pretty negative feelings for me. As a child, the primary feeling I felt was fear. For most of my young life, I had this deep fear of Jesus based on what I learned from the Baptist church. As a kid, I would listen to the minister promote the idea that I was born a sinner and the only way I could get into heaven was to repent for my sins and ask God for forgiveness. Therefore, I was always afraid that God was looking at me and taking notes of everything I did wrong (and there were lots of things I did wrong), and he was waiting for me to die so he could send me straight to hell.

Another feeling I felt quite often was confusion. I simply did not understand how Jesus worked and since I couldn't see him or talk directly to him and ask him some direct questions, I was in a constant state of confusion since no one would answer my questions about him. Another thing that really puzzled me was the fact that all of the pictures I saw of him were white. By the time I got to high school and learned a few things about geography, it didn't make sense to me that being from Jerusalem, Jesus would be a white dude.

If I had to choose one thing that bothered me the most, it would probably be the fact that Jesus was only featured in four chapters of the bible. Since the entire Christian religion was based around Jesus, it seemed odd that he wasn't featured more often in the bible. I remember trying to understand the words in red in the King James Version of the bible, and for the most part, I couldn't understand what he actually taught. The only things I knew for sure was that Jesus was supposed to be the son of God, and God, at the same time, and he died a horrible death for my sins and then he rose from the dead in three days. This really confused me a lot because how could he have died for my sins if he died 2000 years before I was born? I hadn't even committed any sins if I wasn't born during the time he was alive. Talk about confusing!

This chapter intends to try and remove some of the confusion around who Jesus was and share my perception and understanding of his life and mission. As I've mentioned before, I am not an expert or bible scholar, and I do not claim to have all of the answers. What I will be sharing are the answers and conclusions I have come to while doing my research and asking many religious people a lot of questions. The answers I will be sharing will be my "truths" not necessarily "the truth," so if my truths work for you, and resonate with you, then simply incorporate them into your life and use them to improve your life. If they don't, simply discard them and find your own truths. It's really that simple!

One problem I've always had with organized religion is the insistence that there is only one true religion. When I was a member of the Baptist religion, I was taught that it was a sin to listen to or study other religions. Once again, this made absolutely no sense to me. I once asked my minister if it was okay for me to read some books about Buddhism, and he told me I would burn in hell if I did. The scripture he used to justify his comment was from the 10 Commandments in Exodus 20:3, which states, "You shall have no other Gods before me." This is just one of the reasons I left organized religion. Why would God be upset with me for simply wanting to learn about other religions?

With that being said, let me be clear on what I believe about organized religions. I believe all religions originate from the same source and all lead to the same place. (I'll be discussing this in an upcoming chapter.) You can call that source God, The Creator. The Universe, Divine Intelligence, Pure Consciousness or Pure Love. The name really isn't important. What's important is for you to decide whether or not you believe this source is real. Belief is the key that opens the door to your connection to this source. And what is a belief? According to spiritual teacher Abraham Hicks, a belief is simply a thought you think over and over again. So you need to ask yourself what you have been thinking over and over about when it comes to thinking about God. Are those thoughts positive or negative?

Before I begin writing specifically about Jesus, I'd like to share my belief about what author and spiritual teacher Neale Donald Walsch called HEBs, Highly Evolved Beings. Since the beginning of time, several HEBs have shown up on earth to share insights and wisdom to help human beings understand and connect with Divine Intelligence. People like Jesus (Christianity), Buddha (Buddhism), Muhammad (Muslim), Krishna (Hinduism), Abraham (Judaism) were all HEBs that taught humanity how to develop an intimacy and connection with a power greater than themselves. These HEBs are the founders of the five most popular religions of the world. However, did you know there are over four thousand three hundred religions worldwide? This means there are a lot more religious HEBs than just five.

HEBs are not only founders of religions, they can be ordinary human beings who simply choose to take a stand to make the world a better place. People like Martin Luther King Jr., Mahatma Gandhi, Mother Theresa, and Nelson Mandela are examples of HEBs. Any human being that shares insights and wisdom that moves humanity forward by teaching how to connect to Divine Intelligence could be considered an HEB. If you're reading this book, you could be an HEB because that tells me you are committed to your own spiritual growth and evolution, which is something all HEBs have in common. They commit to their own spiritual development, and then they share what they've learned with others.

So, let's talk about Jesus.

It's pretty apparent that he was an HEB. According to the Pew

Research Center, Christianity is the largest religion with the most followers at 2.3 billion. This makes it the most popular religion in the world. The second most popular religion is Islam, with 1.8 billion followers. The third most popular religion is Hinduism with 1.1 billion followers, while Buddhism was fourth with ½ a billion followers and Judaism fifth with 14.7 million followers.

And here is an interesting statistic, 1.2 billion people do not follow any organized religion at all. That is 16% of the world's population. According to another report, Christianity has been experiencing a steady decline over the past twenty years, while people who claim to be agnostic/Atheist have seen a steady increase during that same period.

So does this mean the world is falling into moral decay? Will humanity survive without organized religion?

Here is what I believe.

The decline in organized religion doesn't necessarily mean people are turning away from God. It means people are searching for alternative ways to experience God. As human beings continue to evolve, they are becoming spiritual, not religious. In her book, Conscious Evolution, Barbara Marx Hubbard theorized that human beings are still evolving. She says they are evolving from Homo-Sapiens to Homo-Universalis. This evolution of consciousness is the driving force of why people are searching for ways to create an intimacy and connection to a power greater than themselves. They do not have to participate in organized religion to experience that.

In order to evolve, human beings must be willing to change their minds and learn new things. Here is a powerful quote about what it takes to learn.

"It takes curiosity to learn. It takes courage to unlearn. Learning requires the humility to admit what you don't know today. Unlearning requires the integrity to admit that you were wrong yesterday.

Learning is how you evolve. Unlearning is how you keep up as the world evolves." - Adam Grant

Are you willing to learn? Are you courageous enough to learn some new ideas about Jesus and his teachings?

As mentioned at the beginning of this chapter, when I used to think of Jesus, it brought up lots of negative feelings in me. I had to be willing to unlearn what I was taught about Jesus and relearn some things that now cause me to feel unconditionally loved when I think about him.

What caused me to change my mind and my feelings about him? Here is what I've learned.

First of all, I do believe there was a human being that walked the earth named Jesus. I believe he was the messiah, as mentioned in the bible. I believe he performed miracles, even being resurrected from the dead. I also believe his life should be used as a metaphor for our lives today, and as we follow his teachings, we can gain access to the same Father he referred to in the bible. In doing so, nothing is impossible for us.

I do not believe he is the only way to access Divine Intelligence or God. As I stated earlier, several highly evolved beings have walked this earth that led the way to connect with the Creator. It just so happens that Jesus is the one I'm most familiar with and most comfortable writing about because of my research and my own life experience. I have had several "transcendent experiences" that confirm the presence of "The Christ" within me, and these experiences are the foundation of my spiritual beliefs. My experiences have led me to know without question that there is a Divine Intelligence that created and is still creating this amazing Universe we live in, and I am a divine manifestation of this Divine Intelligence.

Secondly, I used to believe that Christ was Jesus' last name. As a kid, my grandparents would always say Jesus Christ, the ministers would all say Jesus Christ, so I concluded Christ was his last name. What I've learned is there is actually a distinction to be made between Jesus and Christ.

Do you remember what I said in the previous chapter about Christ being the son of God? Christ is the divine energy that God released at the instant the Universe was created. Christ is the divine spark of God that is in every human being. Jesus was the human personality God used to teach us how to access the Christ within each of us. So

Christ wasn't Jesus' last name; Jesus was "The Christed One." He was the ultimate expression of God in human form who attained a level of oneness and connection with Divine Intelligence that he taught was also available to anyone who follows his teachings.

Another quote that confirms this for me comes from John 17:12, in which Jesus says, "While I was with them, I protected them and kept them safe by that name you gave me. None has been lost except the one doomed to destruction so that Scripture would be fulfilled." My interpretation of that passage is there were times throughout the bible when Jesus spoke, and there were times when Christ spoke. In this particular passage, I believe Christ was speaking. When he said, "I kept them safe by that name you gave me," I believe he was talking about the name Jesus. Jesus was the one who was doomed to destruction because Scripture said Jesus would give his life for man.

Making this distinction between Jesus and Christ helps me understand the bible a little better. It allows me to see the story of Jesus through a different lens, and for me, it just makes more sense. Jesus was exactly who he said he was. He was the Son of God prophesied in the Old Testament and the Messiah who was sent to save the world. And yet, he always reminded everyone that they too had the power to do everything he had done.

This is why he said, "I tell you the truth, anyone who has faith in me will do what I have been doing. He will do even greater things than these, because I am going to the Father." (John 14:12) So what exactly did he mean when he said that?

My interpretation is he literally meant what he said. If you look throughout his life, Jesus performed several miracles. He healed the sick, turned water into wine, read people's minds, predicted the future, and ultimately overcame death. So, does this mean human beings can do the same? I believe the answer is yes.

There is a story that talks about a sacred room in one of the temples in Jerusalem that was supposed to be so holy only the highest priests were allowed to go in there. It was so holy that the priests that went in there would tie a rope around their waist just in case if they died while they were in the room, they could be pulled out by people who were not priests. Supposedly there was a very large and beautiful curtain that separated the sacred room from the other rooms.

The story goes that at the exact instance Jesus died on the cross, the curtain split in half, which symbolized that his sacrifice gave every human being direct access to God. I believe that is what he meant when he said, "I am going to the father." When Jesus the human personality died, Christ was released into the world. In John 14:26, Jesus says, "But the Counselor, the Holy Spirit, who the Father will send in my name, will teach you all things and will remind you of everything I have said to you." This confirms for me what I said about the Holy Trinity. There was the Father, which is Divine Intelligence, there was the Son, which is the Christ energy, and there was the Holy Spirit which is the Counselor or, as I stated, the individual expressions of the Son. Put another way, there is the Creator, there is that which was created, which is the Son (The Christ), and there is the individual expression of that which was created. Think back to the metaphor about the ocean. We are all divine expressions of the ocean.

Another thing that Jesus said that confirms the distinction between Jesus and Christ can be found in John 17:5 when he said, "And now Father, glorify me in your presence with the glory I had with you before the world began." So, I'd like you to think about that comment for a moment. Based on the bible, we know that Jesus was only in his 30's. How is it possible for Jesus to have been with God before the world began? Remember at the beginning when there was only nothingness and then something came from nothing? Where would Jesus have been? On the other hand, if Christ is the son, isn't it possible for it to have been with God before the world began? I believe the answer is yes, and that is why I believe there is a distinction between Jesus the personality and Christ. I'll say it once again, Jesus was the personality through which Divine Intelligence demonstrated and expressed the Son, which is Christ. Does this make sense to you?

If you study the life of Jesus, you will find that there is nowhere in the bible where he took credit for any of the miracles he performed. Whenever he performed a miracle, he would either say, "It is not I but my father within that does the work," or he would say, "it is your faith that healed you." Jesus recognized that he was not the Source of the healings and miracles; his Father was.

And yet, the majority of Christians still worship Jesus even though he told them not to. In Mark 10:45, he said, "For even the son of man did not come to be served, but to serve." Once again, he clarifies that The Creator, Divine Intelligence, or God, is the source, not him.

I do not believe making a distinction between Jesus and Christ in any way diminishes Jesus' life or his teachings. God needed to speak in a way that human beings could understand, so he took the form of a man so we could know that it was real.

Another lesson I've learned about Jesus that puts my mind and heart at ease is that Jesus did not die for my sins. I realize this goes against traditional Christian teachings, but I am absolutely certain it is an erroneous teaching. Seeing Jesus nailed on the cross used to bring up feelings of guilt and shame for me because I believed the traditional teaching that Jesus died for my sins; therefore, I felt partly responsible for his death. If you've ever watched the Passion of the Christ movie by Mel Gibson, you may have had the same experience I had. I was heartbroken and saddened and could barely watch the movie because of its brutality, and yet as I watched it, I somehow felt like it was partially my fault that he was killed.

So what was the purpose of Jesus' death? I believe his purpose was to show the world the infinite power that comes from being intimately connected to Divine Intelligence. In other words, Jesus' death and resurrection symbolize that God is all-powerful and can transcend anything, even death. When we surrender to the Infinite power of God, nothing is impossible. Jesus' entire message was about having faith in his Father and recognizing that faith is the key that opens the door to accessing his Father's power. I like to think of this power as Source Energy. Source energy is what drives everything in the Universe. Jesus' death is what launched the Christian movement. Without it, Christianity wouldn't exist.

Another lesson I learned from Jesus is that you do not have to die to get into heaven. I'm sure you've heard the story of streets paved with gold and angels playing harps in heaven. Most Christian religions teach that your goal is to be good while you are here on earth so that when you die, you will be rewarded by going to heaven. The key is, you have to die before you get into heaven. I do not believe that is true. I believe you can experience heaven right here on earth, and Jesus came to teach you exactly how to do this. By his own admission, you don't have to die to get into heaven. In Matthew 16:28, Jesus said, "Truly I tell you, some who are standing here will not taste death before they see the Son of Man coming in his kingdom." There are many different interpretations of this passage. I read it to say you do not have to die before you enter the kingdom of God, and therefore, it's possible for you to experience heaven on earth.

So, what was Jesus' mission on earth? For me, I believe he showed up to confirm there really is a Creator of the Universe. He showed up to teach us how to access Divine Intelligence and develop intimacy and connection to his "Father." In doing so, we would experience the unconditional love of a loving Creator, and by following Jesus' example, we could literally create heaven on earth. His ultimate message is God is Love, and we all have direct access to that love.

When Jesus was asked which was the greatest commandment, his reply was, "Love the Lord your God with all your heart and with all your soul and with all your mind. This is the first and greatest commandment. And the second is like it: 'Love your neighbor as yourself.' All the Law and the Prophets hang on these two commandments." Matthew 22:37-40

Knowing this truth is what changed my thoughts and feelings about Jesus. No longer do I feel anger or confusion about him or his life. As I've said several times throughout this book, this is my "truth," it's how I see Jesus and his mission.

In the title, I asked the question, "What If Jesus Were a Coach?" and it is my contention that he was a coach. As a matter of fact, he was the greatest life coach that has ever walked this earth. Therefore, I study his life and his teachings and try to emulate his actions to the best of my ability so that I gain access to the Father so that nothing is impossible for me. My tagline on my website says, "I am an irrepressible optimist with a passion for the impossible." I chose that tagline because it follows one of the most powerful messages I've received from Coach Jesus, "I can do all things through Christ who strengthens me." Christ is the divine energy of the Universe, and when you gain access to it, you too will believe anything is possible.

Christianity is the most widely practiced religion in the world, with more than 2 billion followers. The Christian faith centers on beliefs regarding the birth, life, death, and resurrection of Jesus Christ. While it started with a small group of adherents, many historians regard the spread and adoption of Christianity throughout the world as one of the most successful spiritual missions in human history.

CHAPTER 4
What Is Christianity?

According to traditional Christianity, if you repent of your sins and confess with your mouth that Jesus is your Lord and savior, you are immediately saved, and you become a Christian. When I was forced to be baptized as a child, I remember the minister asking me if I accepted Jesus as my Lord and savior and the only reason I said yes was because I was basically coerced into saying it.

When I went back to church after my divorce, I volunteered to be saved and repented my sins and accepted Jesus as my Lord and savior. I remember giving my testimony of how Jesus had come into my life and turned it around and then hearing the whole church burst into applause because of my sharing. But even as I stood there listening to their cheers, deep down inside, I knew I wasn't being honest with myself. A part of me really didn't believe in God, and I really couldn't wrap my mind around why I needed to be "saved" in the first place.

What I realize in retrospect is that sharing my testimony in church and accepting Jesus as my Lord and savior were really about gaining approval from the church. I had been deeply depressed and isolated after my divorce, and having the church applaud and accept me into the church made me feel better and removed my feelings of loneliness. It actually had nothing to do with accepting Jesus into my heart.

As I mentioned in a previous chapter, eventually, I had to be willing to be honest with myself about what I truly believed. And ultimately, I came to a conclusion at one point that I honestly didn't believe in God.

What I honestly could not understand was why God would require us to repent of our sins to be saved? Since he said we were made in his image and after his likeness and that image and likeness was spirit, wasn't that the ultimate contradiction? If you were born in his image, and he said you were born a sinner, wouldn't that make him a sinner also?

Too many questions, yet so few answers.

So, what does it mean to be "Christian" and what exactly is "Christianity?"

For me, I believe Christianity is a process we go through to become Christlike. If we follow the teachings of Jesus and realize that his life is a metaphor for us to follow, and then apply the lessons he taught us to our own lives, we then become connected to our Christ nature, and nothing is impossible for us to be, do, or have.

So how do we do this?

I'd like to share a chapter from one of my previous books: *Adversity Is Your Greatest Ally*. The chapter is titled; The Hero's Journey. It is based on a theory by a man named Joseph Campbell. Joseph theorized that as human beings, we are all heroes. There are 12 stages of the hero's journey, and to understand this truth, we must all go on our own individual hero's journey. He used the term monomyth to explain how most movies were based on the concept of the hero's journey mythology. One of the most famous movies based on the hero's journey is Star Wars, which to this day is still my all-time favorite movie. In this chapter, I share how I went on my own personal hero's journey and how it helped shape my life.

After I share that chapter and my story, I will explain how Jesus' life goes through the hero's journey and how Christianity actually follows the 12 stages of the Hero's Journey.

Back in 1977 (I was 17 at the time), a friend and I were hanging out late one night and decided we would check out a movie. Neither of us knew what movie we wanted to see, so we began looking at the theatre's movie posters. I then noticed a poster for a new sci-fi movie that had recently been released, and based on the poster, it looked pretty interesting. We decided to go and check it out, even though we knew nothing about the movie.

> From the very beginning of the movie, I knew it was going to be special. I was instantly transported into outer space, and the story, actors, visuals, and soundtrack were all out of this world. By the time the movie was over, I had been on an amazing journey that I didn't want to end. I loved the movie so much that I convinced my friend to go back the following night to see it again.
>
> During that summer, I ended up watching the movie more than twenty times in the theater. I couldn't stop watching it. Each time I watched it, I discovered something new, and after each viewing, I couldn't wait to see it again.
>
> It may sound a little odd, but the movie somehow changed my life. It gave me a new perception of reality, and as a result of watching it so many times, my attitude changed about the Universe and my place within it. The movie was Star Wars, and even today, it is my all-time favorite movie. I still watch it once or twice a year.
>
> The most intriguing concept of the movie was "The Force," which was defined as a universal energy that is within all things and controls all things. The primary character of the movie is Luke Skywalker, and the movie follows him as he learns how to access The Force within him and how he ultimately uses it to save humanity from an evil character named Darth Vader, who used The Force for evil, unlike Luke, who used the force for good.
>
> After the movie came out, what caught my attention was the number of religious leaders who were using the movie to promote their religion and were actually referring to "The Force" as a metaphor for their God. During this time, I was more of an agnostic and I really didn't believe in God; the non-religious message in the movie actually attracted me. I resonated with the idea that every human being has access to this Force, and you didn't have to be religious to connect with it. You simply had to

learn how to access it and believe in it, and it would become a source of amazing abilities and powers.

I had been doing some research about science and physics, and there were some fascinating ideas that I had been exposed to that seemed to confirm what The Force in the movie was actually talking about. It reminded me of a famous quote from Albert Einstein (my favorite scientist) in which he stated, "Everything is energy that's just the way that it is. Match the frequency of the reality that you want to create and there is no way that you can't create that reality. It can be no other way. This isn't philosophy, this is physics."

My interpretation of this quote is that The Force is the divine energy of the Universe. It is the animating force of life, and it is actually the Source of all things. I believe every human being has direct access to this energy, and it is our responsibility to learn how to access it and use it for our highest good.

Approximately twenty years after falling in love with Star Wars, I discovered what it was that compelled me to have such a deep connection and infatuation with the movie.

I was flipping through the channels on television, and I ran across an interview between Bill Moyers and a man named Joseph Campbell. Mr. Campbell was a mythologist who had been studying religion, philosophy, and science, and he created a theory that he called the mono-myth. His theory suggested that the overwhelming majority of movies/myths contained a common theme or story. He coined the term *The Hero's Journey* to explain his theory.

As I listened to the interview, I had the same feeling of fascination and wonderment that I had when I watched Star Wars for the very first time. I was absolutely entranced with his ideas and belief systems, which were definitely congruent with my own. It turns out that Star Wars was based on Mr. Campbell's theory of the Hero's Journey. His work had a huge impact on the creator of Star Wars, George Lucas. As Mr. Campbell explained his theory and philosophy, my love and fascination with Star Wars deepened, and the reason why I loved it became abundantly clear.

Although I didn't recognize it at the time, I had already begun my own Hero's Journey. I had intuitively recognized the deeper meaning in the movie, and there was a part of me that knew that I would one day become aware of this journey and ultimately use the theory as the foundation for creating the life of my dreams.

After listening to the interview, I began reading more about Mr. Campbell and his theory. I have to credit him with being a mentor and resource of motivation and inspiration as I learned how to use his 12 stages of the Hero's Journey to help me rebuild my life.

Learning how to apply his theory to my own life really supported me in turning my adversities into allies, and I am deeply grateful that I was introduced to his work. His theory has so powerfully impacted my life that I have chosen to include it in this book because I know that once embraced, becoming aware of your own Hero's Journey can become a powerful and positive source of wisdom that will guide you to live the life you were born to live.

To do this, you must understand and accept a very simple premise. You are a Hero, and whether you believe it or not, you are on a journey. The question you must ask yourself right now is, are you willing to become conscious of the journey you're on, or are you going to stay unconscious? The fact that you are reading these words right now at this particular time tells me that you are ready to become conscious and are ready to embark on your own Hero's Journey. Now, I would like to share the 12 stages of the Hero's Journey to support you along the way.

To support you in fully understanding the journey, I will share some insights I've gained over the past twenty years of my own journey. As you read the 12 stages and then my commentary, take a moment to reflect on both. See if you recognize any similarities in your own life and try to identify where you are on your journey.

What If Jesus Were A Coach?

1. Ordinary World

This is where the Hero exists before his present story begins, oblivious of the adventures to come. It's his safe place. His everyday life where we learn crucial details about our Hero, his true nature, capabilities, and outlook on life. This anchors the Hero as a human, just like you and me, and makes it easier for us to identify with him and hence later, empathize with his plight.

> At this stage in my own life, I was trapped on the societal rollercoaster. I was 23-years-old, and I had done everything society said I was supposed to do to be successful. All of my energy was focused on making money and accumulating material things. I had worked extremely hard to climb the corporate ladder, and I had been rewarded with a great salary, purchasing my first home, and having a wife and kids. Although it looked like I had the ideal life on the outside, in my heart and mind, I knew something was missing. But I didn't have a clue what that something was.

2. Call to Adventure

The Hero's adventure begins when he receives a call to action, such as a direct threat to his safety, his family, his way of life, or to the peace of the community in which he lives. It may not be as dramatic as a gunshot, but simply a phone call or conversation, but whatever the call is, and however it manifests itself, it ultimately disrupts the comfort of the Hero's Ordinary World and presents a challenge or quest that must be undertaken.

> My call to adventure began at the age of 29. My American Dream had turned into a nightmare as I experienced the pain, humiliation, and frustration of a divorce, bankruptcy, foreclosure, and a deep state of depression. It was the darkest, difficult, and challenging time of my life. There were times when the pain was so great that I even contemplated taking my own life. Despite the pain and suffering I experienced, I now realize that this is the time in my life when I received my call to adventure. A part of me intuitively knew that I wasn't living up to my full potential, and I

finally realized just how unhappy I was with my life. I refer to my divorce as my wake-up call, and now in retrospect, I can clearly see that my divorce and all of the pain I experienced were actually the best things that could have happened to me.

3. Refusal of the Call

Although the Hero may be eager to accept the quest, at this stage, he will have fears that need overcoming. Second thoughts or even deep personal doubts as to whether or not he is up to the challenge. When this happens, the Hero will refuse the call, and as a result, may suffer somehow. The problem he faces may seem too much to handle and the comfort of home far more attractive than the perilous road ahead. This would also be our own response and once again helps us bond further with the reluctant Hero.

After my divorce, my primary focus was to simply put my life back together. I had to confront the fact that I was unhappy in my career, and I was truly ready to do something different with my life. Although it appeared to be irrational at the time, I decided to quit my job and start my own company. Unfortunately, things did not go the way I planned, and after approximately six months, I was in even worse shape. My life was spiraling out of control, and I couldn't see a way out.

4. Meeting the Mentor

At this crucial turning point where the Hero desperately needs guidance, he meets a mentor figure who gives him something he needs. He could be given an object of great importance, insight into the dilemma he faces, wise advice, practical training, or even self-confidence. Whatever the mentor provides the Hero with serves to dispel his doubts and fears and give him the strength and courage to begin his quest.

I reached a point in my life where I had two choices; get help or die. There was no gray area. I was in such deep emotional, psychological, and physical pain that I knew that I could no longer deal with it all on my own. I gained the courage to go to therapy and

> began my internal journey of transformation. My therapist was able to help me identify the cause of a lot of my dysfunctional behavior, and she gave me some insights that helped me alleviate my depression. I eventually began to feel happy and hopeful again.

5. Crossing The Threshold

The Hero is now ready to act upon his call to adventure and truly begin his quest, whether it be physical, spiritual, or emotional. He may go willingly or he may be pushed, but either way, he finally crosses the threshold between the world he is familiar with and that which he is not. It may be leaving home for the first time in his life or just doing something he has always been scared to do. However the threshold presents itself, this action signifies the Hero's commitment to his journey and whatever it may have in store for him.

> Going to therapy opened up a whole new world to me. It helped me recognize that all my life, I had been focused on things outside of myself, things like money, titles, material things, and other people's approval. I learned that I needed to focus on what's inside of me, like my thoughts, feelings and beliefs, if I truly wanted to be happy.
>
> As a result, I became committed to understanding myself from the inside out, so I immersed myself in the study of psychology, philosophy, spirituality, and personal development.

6. Tests, Allies, Enemies

Now finally out of his comfort zone, the Hero is confronted with an ever more difficult series of challenges that test him in a variety of ways. Obstacles are thrown across his path; whether they be physical hurdles or people bent on thwarting his progress, the Hero must overcome each challenge he is presented with on the journey towards his ultimate goal.

The Hero needs to find out who can be trusted and who can't. He may earn allies and meet enemies who will, each in their own way, help prepare him for the greater ordeals yet to come. This is the stage where his skills and/or powers are tested, and every obstacle that he faces helps us to gain a deeper insight into his character and ultimately identify with him further.

> After therapy, I needed to continue my growth, so I began participating in a wide variety of personal development seminars. During the seminars, I was challenged to address my internal fears and doubts about myself. What really helped me grow was my willingness to allow other people to support and encourage me. I learned that I had a huge issue with trust, and by being willing to work with others, I learned how to trust again.

The inmost cave may represent many things in the Hero's story such as an actual location in which lies a terrible danger or an inner conflict which up until now the Hero has not had to face. As the Hero approaches the cave, he must make final preparations before taking that final leap into the great unknown.

At the threshold to the inmost cave, the Hero may once again face some of the doubts and fears that first surfaced upon his call to adventure. He may need some time to reflect upon his journey and the treacherous road ahead in order to find the courage to continue. This brief respite helps the audience understand the magnitude of the ordeal that awaits the Hero and escalates the tension in anticipation of his ultimate test.

> After a few years of workshops and reading a few hundred books, I was at a point in my life where I was feeling pretty good about myself, and I had started rebuilding my life. It hadn't been easy, but all of my hard work had paid off. My relationships were real and authentic; I felt happy and whole within myself. I had found a job that provided some financial stability, and I was pretty optimistic about my future and life in general. But despite this, something was missing. I couldn't put my finger on it, but internally I knew there was something more I needed to do.

8. Ordeal

The Supreme Ordeal may be a dangerous physical test or a deep inner crisis that the Hero must face in order to survive, or for the world in which the Hero lives to continue to exist. Whether it be facing his greatest fear or most deadly foe, the Hero must draw upon all of his skills and his experiences gathered upon the path to the inmost cave in order to overcome his most difficult challenge.

Only through some form of "death" can the Hero be reborn, experiencing a metaphorical resurrection that somehow grants him greater power or insight necessary in order to fulfill his destiny or reach his journey's end. This is the high-point of the Hero's story and where everything he holds dear is put on the line. If he fails, he will either die or live as he knows it will never be the same again.

> During my transformation journey, I came upon a book by John Bradshaw that would change my life forever. The book was *Healing The Shame That Binds You*, and after reading it, I knew I had found the missing piece of my life's puzzle. What I learned from the book was that my actions had been driven by a deep feeling of shame all my life. It was shame that had driven me to be successful. It was also shame that kept me from creating intimacy and connection in my relationships. It was shame that kept me isolated from others and didn't allow me to truly trust anyone. It was a deep feeling of shame that kept me trapped in my own private prison and kept me from expressing who I really am.
>
> I decided that I wanted to remove that shame, and I chose to participate in a workshop with John Bradshaw called *Healing Your Inner Child*. During this workshop, I learned how my abusive childhood was the source of my feelings of shame. I had to allow myself to go back and experience the pain and trauma of those earlier events in my life in order to move past the shame. During the process, I learned how the abuse I experienced caused me to disconnect from my emotions, and by allowing myself to feel them, I could then begin the process of healing. This emotional healing process is what allowed me to become free of the shame. By releasing my shame and forgiving myself, I opened the door to emotional freedom, and I was able to complete my life's puzzle and move forward with my life.

9. Reward (Seizing the sword)

After defeating the enemy, surviving death, and finally overcoming his greatest personal challenge, the Hero is ultimately transformed into a new state, emerging from battle as a stronger person and often with a prize.

The Reward may come in many forms: an object of great importance or power, a secret, greater knowledge or insight, or even reconciliation with a loved one or ally. Whatever the treasure, which may well facilitate his return to the Ordinary World, the Hero must quickly put celebrations aside and prepare for the last leg of his journey.

After my experience with the inner child work, everything changed for the better. For the first time in my life, I felt whole and complete. I no longer sought out exterior validation because I was happy and content with who I am as a human being. My shame was replaced with a deep self-confidence, and I learned how to accept myself and love myself unconditionally. This was definitely my greatest gift - learning to love myself just for the man that I am.

10. The Road Back

This stage in the Hero's journey represents a reverse echo of the Call to Adventure in which the Hero had to cross the first threshold. Now he must return home with his reward, but this time the anticipation of danger is replaced with that of acclaim and perhaps vindication, absolution, or even exoneration.

But the Hero's journey is not yet over, and he may still need one last push back into the Ordinary World. The moment before the Hero finally commits to the last stage of his journey may be a moment in which he must choose between his own personal objective and that of a Higher Cause.

> As a result of doing my inner work, I concluded that I wanted to share the lessons I learned about myself with others. Although I had no writing experience or training, I decided that I would begin writing books in the hopes to inspire others. I have also learned that in writing books and sharing lessons with others, I continue to learn and grow. The road of life has lots of twists and

turns, and sometimes all we need are some guideposts along the way, which is why I have chosen to be a writer. Writing helps me return home to my true self while guiding others to do the same.

11. Resurrection

This is the climax in which the Hero must have his final and most dangerous encounter with death. The final battle also represents something far greater than the Hero's own existence, with its outcome having far-reaching consequences to his Ordinary World and the lives of those he left behind.

If he fails, others will suffer, and this not only places more weight upon his shoulders but in a movie, grips the audience so that they too feel part of the conflict and share the Hero's hopes, fears, and trepidation. Ultimately the Hero will succeed, destroy his enemy, and emerge from battle cleansed and reborn.

> When I first began writing, I had to face a multitude of fears. What if nobody reads my books? What if they read them and don't like them? What gives me the right to write and publish a book? Who am I to think that I can be a successful author? Since I don't have any credentials, will I be ridiculed and attacked?
>
> All of these fears were unwarranted. By being willing to face my fears and move past any preconceived ideas I had about what it takes to be an author, I learned that I no longer needed anyone else's approval or permission to do what I love to do. I love writing! I love being an author! That's it, end of story! As a writer, I simply must write because it's what's inside me. Even if I never sold a single book or no one ever reads my writings, I would still write because I have to, because it is a creative outlet that I have to express.
>
> If I had not heeded my call to adventure, I would probably still be stuck on that societal rollercoaster, and I would have never discovered my gift for writing. So all of the struggles and challenges that I overcame helped me resurrect the gift of writing that had always been dormant within me.

A part of me died during this process, yet the real me was resurrected, and it was worth all the pain and suffering I had endured along the way.

12. Return with the Elixir

This is the final stage of the Hero's journey in which he returns home to his Ordinary World, a changed man. He will have grown as a person, learned many things, faced many terrible dangers, and even death, but now looks forward to the start of a new life. His return may bring fresh hope to those he left behind, a direct solution to their problems, or perhaps a new perspective for everyone to consider.

The final reward that he obtains may be literal or metaphoric. It could be a cause for celebration, self-realization, or an end to strife, but whatever it is, it represents three things: change, success, and proof of his journey. The return home also signals the need for resolution for the story's other key players. The Hero's doubters will be ostracized, his enemies punished, and his allies rewarded. Ultimately, the Hero will return to where he started, but things will clearly never be the same again.

As I reflect over my twenty-year journey of transformation, it is nothing short of a miracle. I could have never imagined the joy and gratitude I feel daily as a result of going on my own hero's journey. By accepting my own call and trusting my inner wisdom, I awakened to my own divine purpose and discovered some unique gifts and talents I have that allow me to support others in their journey. That's very rewarding and fulfilling for me. I took the road less traveled, and it has made all the difference in my life and the lives of others.

I have come to accept that the Hero's Journey isn't just a theory; it is a step-by-step process of discovering who you really are and why you are here. At some point, every human being must engage in their own journey, and each one is as unique as our fingerprints. No two are exactly the same.

It begins with your acceptance of a very simple fact - you are indeed a hero, and therefore you are already engaged in the hero's

> journey, whether you realize it or not. By becoming aware of this fact and following these 12 stages, I believe you can begin and finish your own Hero's Journey.
>
> Rest assured that it may not be easy, but I guarantee it will be worth it.
>
> If you're interested in going deeper, I highly recommend that you pick up a copy of Joseph Campbell's book *The Hero With A Thousand Faces*. It's a fascinating read that explains the hero's journey in more detail. If you can find the interview with Bill Moyers and Joseph Campbell, do yourself a favor and watch it!
>
> I also recommend that you pick up a copy or watch the movie *Finding Joe* by Patrick Takaya Solomon. It is a beautiful film that illustrates how the Hero's Journey works, and has some great insights from various experts on the Hero's Journey theory.
>
> You can also Google The Hero's Journey and get infinite information and resources to learn more.

I want to close this chapter with a quote.

"It's not what happens to you that matters, it's how you respond to what happens to you that makes all the difference in the world."

May The Force Be With You!

Every human being is unique and different, and so too is the Hero's Journey. No one can go on your journey for you; you have to go on it yourself. Rest assured you already have everything you need inside of you to begin your journey, so the only thing that is missing is your commitment to start. Are you willing to begin your Hero's Journey?

To support you on your journey, I would like to share how Jesus's life followed the Hero's Journey and how Christianity is actually based on the 12 stages of the Hero's Journey. Therefore, becoming a Christian is a lot more than just repenting your sins and accepting

Jesus as your Lord and savior. Becoming a Christian is a process you must go through, just like Jesus. It is a transformational process that was put in place by Divine Intelligence, and it was designed to support you in transforming from who you thought you were to who you were born to be. Put another way, the journey is designed to empower you to become Christ-like, just like Jesus.

Now let's review Jesus' life through the lens of the Hero's Journey.

Ordinary World -1

We all know the story of Jesus being born in a manger wrapped in swaddling clothing to parents with very modest means. I believe this is important because it symbolizes that you do not have to be born with great wealth to do great things. Material things and external wealth are not required to fulfil God's purpose for your life. Jesus' life teaches us that everything we need to do God's work and fulfill our unique purpose is already inside us when we are born. We do not need anything "outside" of us to express our divinity. All we need to do is access the Christ within, and nothing is impossible for us. Therefore, we are born in an ordinary world, but we can do extraordinary things by connecting to Divine Intelligence.

Call To Adventure – 2

In the bible, Jesus begins preaching around the age of 12. He accepted his call to adventure by starting his ministry at this very young age. He intuitively knew he was called to share the "truth" about his father, and therefore, he trusted his inner wisdom and launched a movement that changed the world.

Refusal Of The Call - 3

There are several gaps in the bible about Jesus' life. Some people theorize that he chose to work as a carpenter during his teenage and early adulthood years. Since there is so little information concerning his early life, one could conclude that he temporarily refused his call to ministry by doing carpentry work. The majority of Jesus' life story focuses on his life in his 30's, so it is conceivable that he refused the call in his late teens and late twenty's.

Meeting The Mentor – 4

Mark 1:1-8 says, "*The beginning of the good news about Jesus the Messiah, the Son of God, as it is written in Isaiah the prophet:*

"I will send my messenger ahead of you, who will prepare your way a voice of one calling in the wilderness, Prepare the way for the Lord, make straight paths for him."

And so John the Baptist appeared in the wilderness, preaching a baptism of repentance for the forgiveness of sins. The whole Judean countryside and all the people of Jerusalem went out to him. Confessing their sins, they were baptized by him in the Jordan River. John wore clothing made of camel's hair, with a leather belt around his waist, and he ate locusts and wild honey. And this was his message: "After me comes the one more powerful than I, the straps of whose sandals I am not worthy to stoop down and untie. I baptize you with water, but he will baptize you with the Holy Spirit."

This is the passage that introduced water baptism to the Christian faith.

When Jesus first met John the Baptist, he initially refused to baptize him. He knew Jesus was the Messiah, and he didn't deem himself worthy enough to do it. But Jesus convinced him to do it, and after John baptized him, as Jesus was coming out of the water, John saw heaven being torn open and the spirit descended on Jesus like a dove, and a voice came from heaven and said, "You are my son, whom I love; with you I am well pleased".

John the Baptist was the meeting of the mentor for Jesus.

Crossing The Threshold - 5

When Jesus began preaching, the priest and rabbis confronted him and accused him of being a false prophet. They did not believe he was the messiah, and they constantly asked him questions to try and understand where his knowledge and wisdom came from. As Jesus answered their questions, they were constantly embarrassed and bewildered by Jesus' deep understanding of the word of God. As Jesus continued to preach, more and more people began to listen to him, and they then began believing he was definitely the messiah, and his ministry began growing exponentially. At this point, he crossed the threshold from being Jesus the carpenter's son to Jesus the Messiah.

Tests, Allies, Enemies - 6

Matthew 4:1-11 says, *"Then Jesus was led by the Spirit into the wilderness to be tempted by the devil. After fasting forty days and forty nights, he was hungry. The tempter came to him and said, "If you are the Son of God, tell these stones to become bread."*

Jesus answered, "It is written: 'Man shall not live on bread alone, but on every word that comes from the mouth of God.'"

Then the devil took him to the holy city and had him stand on the highest point of the temple. "If you are the Son of God," he said, "throw yourself down. For it is written:

"'He will command his angels concerning you, and they will lift you up in their hands, so that you will not strike your foot against a stone.'"

Jesus answered him, "It is also written: 'Do not put the Lord your God to the test.'"

Again, the devil took him to a very high mountain and showed him all the kingdoms of the world and their splendor. "All this I will give you," he said, "if you will bow down and worship me."

Jesus said to him, "Away from me, Satan! For it is written: 'Worship the Lord your God, and serve him only.'"

Then the devil left him, and angels came and attended him.

The devil tempted Jesus, and he passed the test and was rewarded with angels. As he grew his ministry, he then chose 12 disciples to become his allies and to help spread his message. One of his disciples betrayed him and became his enemy. Yet, Jesus understood that his betrayal was actually a part of God's plan for his life, and he accepted the betrayal and even forgave the disciple who betrayed him.

Approach To The Inmost Cave – 7

During his 40 days in the wilderness, Jesus spent time in quiet contemplation and meditation, thinking about his purpose and mission in life. This gave him time to develop an intimacy and connection with his Father. During that time, he was isolated from others, which symbolizes how we must take the time to disconnect from others, allowing us to connect with Divine Intelligence. There is a wonderful scene in the movie Star Wars in which the main character, Luke Skywalker, is being trained by his mentor, Yoda. Yoda tells Luke that he has to enter this dark cave as part of his training. When Luke asks Yoda what's in the cave, Yoda replies: "only what you take with you." The inmost cave is our own mind, and we must be willing to get rid of any darkness that may be inside our minds.

Ordeal – 8

Jesus was tortured and crucified for claiming to be the Messiah. At any point, he could have chosen to deny his claim and been released. Yet, he accepted the consequences knowing that everything he was going through was part of God's plan, and ultimately, he would be able to glorify his Father. He accepted his ordeal with the faith that his father was always present, and as difficult as it was, he knew with absolute certainty that he had to give his life to save humanity.

Reward – 9

Jesus knew by giving his own life, he would provide access to his father to anyone who believed in him. He understood his divine purpose, and knowing he was doing his Father's will was his reward. This is what unconditional love looks like—loving humanity so much that he was willing to sacrifice his life for all of humanity.

Chapter 4: What Is Christianity?

The Road Back - 10

After Jesus was crucified on the cross, he was placed in a tomb for three days. On the third day, he was resurrected. The story says that initially, after his resurrection, Mary Magdalene was sitting at his tomb crying when he appeared and said, (John 20:17) *"Do not hold on to me, for I have not yet returned to the Father. Go instead to my brothers and tell them I am returning to my Father and your Father, to my God and your God."* Jesus understood he had to return to his father first to fulfill his divine mission, and then he would come back to prove to the world that he had fulfilled the prophecy and confirm he was the son of God. This was Jesus' road back to his Father, which symbolizes how we must each return home to connect with Divine Intelligence.

Resurrection – 11

Being resurrected from the dead was the ultimate expression of the power of God. But his resurrection symbolizes how we must allow certain parts of our ego to die for us to be resurrected in spirit. This is the essence of Christianity and becoming Christlike. We must die of the flesh and be resurrected in the spirit.

Return With The Elixir - 12

When Jesus ascended into heaven, he knew that his spirit would live on through the holy spirit. By sacrificing his life, he gave humanity a blueprint of how God worked, and he knew if anyone would embrace his teachings and follow his example, they too could gain access to his Father. So the elixir Jesus returned with is the unconditional love of God, and he shared that love with us by sacrificing his life so that we could all have access to it.

Take a moment and think about your own life right now. Are you willing to begin your own hero's journey? From my own experience, I will say there is nothing that compares to the joy and inner peace I experience daily due to my own hero's journey. It has nothing to do with religious dogma or doctrine, and you do not have to go to any specific building to start your journey. All you have to do is commit to your own inner transformation and growth and then learn to trust that still small voice inside of you that will guide you along the way. Hopefully, this chapter has provided you with some insights on what to expect.

Rest assured that you already have everything you need inside of you to begin and complete your journey. All you need is the commitment, courage, patience, and persistence to begin, and then you will have to learn how to trust Divine Intelligence to guide you on your way.

I believe in you! You can do this!

I will close this chapter with a simple idea, Christianity is the process of becoming Christlike. It's a lot more than just wearing a label called Christian, and repenting your sins and accepting Jesus as your lord and savior. It's about transforming your mind and heart to be just like Jesus. By following in his footsteps, we can gain access to the Father, and nothing will be impossible for us.

Good luck on your journey!

"Jesus was not a Christian
Buddha was not a Buddhist
Muhammed was not a Muslim
They were all teachers, and what they taught was love!
Love was their religion."

- Author unknown

CHAPTER 5
My Favorite Lessons From The Master

Have you ever had a teacher or a coach who believed in you so strongly that it encouraged you to believe in yourself and their encouragement helped you reach your fullest potential? I'm absolutely certain you have. Maybe it was a teacher or athletic coach, perhaps your parent, an uncle, or even a close friend. I'm sure you can think of someone who you would consider to be your favorite teacher.

There is a wonderful saying that goes, "When the student is ready, the teacher will appear." For me, that teacher was Ms. Bussey. She was my elementary school teacher back in 1967-1971. I absolutely loved Ms. Bussey!

When I was six years old, I had to go live with my grandparents because my oldest sister had a brain tumor, and she was in and out of hospitals for several years. Since my mom was a single parent of six kids, she could not handle the financial burden of all of us, so she sent me and my older brother and sister to live with my father's parents. We were there for seven years, and I considered it my seven years of hell. It was seven years of physical, emotional, psychological, and sexual abuse that no child should have had to experience.

Ms. Bussey was my saving grace. She knew of the abusive

environment I was in, and she went out of her way to nurture me emotionally and intellectually. She told me that the key to my success was my intellect, and she challenged me to get good grades and stay out of trouble. Even though it's been more than 53 years since I've spoken with or seen her, I still cherish the lessons and guidance she gave me, and I am forever grateful that she believed in me and challenged me to become the best version of myself.

One of the fastest-growing industries in the world is the coaching industry. Coaching is just another form of teaching. There are life coaches, relationship coaches, financial coaches, health coaches, parenting coaches, mindset coaches, etc. No matter what you want to learn, coaches are available to teach you anything you're interested in learning.

So what do coaches do?

To answer that question, I'd like you to think about one of your favorite athletes. Is it Michael Jordan, Tiger Woods, Tom Brady, Michael Phelps, Serena Williams, or maybe Simone Biles? These are some of the greatest athletes in the world, and the one thing they all have in common is they rely on their coaches to be the best they can be.

A coach's job is to help bring out all of the potentials within their student. They can help the athlete identify areas in their game where they can improve. They teach, encourage, motivate, inspire, and challenge the athlete to reach their fullest potential.

This book is another form of coaching. It provides you with insights that can support you in becoming the best version of yourself. The fact that you're reading this book tells me you are open to coaching and you are willing to learn how to become the best version of yourself.

Unfortunately, very few people are open to coaching. Most people are unwilling to learn new things because it is uncomfortable, and the majority of people have an aversion to discomfort. But here is a very important coaching lesson you must be willing to accept. If something doesn't challenge you, it can't change you. In other words, you must be willing to get out of your comfort zones if you are truly committed to your own personal growth and development.

Chapter 5: My Favorite Lessons From The Master

Rest assured, this book is going to expand your comfort zones. There will definitely be things that will challenge your way of thinking. It may be a little uncomfortable at first, but rest assured, embracing some new ways of thinking can definitely change your life for the better if you stick with it.

In this chapter, I'd like to share some of my favorite life lessons I've learned from the teachings of Jesus. I personally believe Jesus was the greatest spiritual coach that has ever lived. If you embrace his teachings without the religious dogma and doctrine of most organized religions, I can assure you his teachings can help transform your life.

In a previous chapter, I mentioned several highly evolved beings that have walked the earth. My research has led me to believe each of these beings shared the same message. That message is, all human beings have access to Divine Intelligence or God. This Divine Intelligence is inherent in all things. Another name for this Intelligence is Love. Love is the animating force of life. It is the highest vibration of energy in the Universe. It is literally God.

Jesus came to teach us how to love!

After studying the five major religions of the world, I have come to the conclusion that Jesus was the ultimate expression of God in human form. I don't think that makes him better than other spiritual teachers. It simply means he is the one I most resonate with and have studied the most. I'd like to share a story with you to explain why Jesus is my favorite spiritual teacher.

I mentioned earlier that I used to be an Atheist. I also said that I decided to find my own truth about God, which led me on this amazing spiritual journey. One of the most amazing experiences of this spiritual journey occurred late one night as I was reading a book titled Living Buddha, Living Christ by Thich Nhat Hanh. In the book, he talked about the parallel messages of Jesus and Buddha. I was pleasantly surprised to learn how similar their messages were, and after reading that book, I decided to learn more about the teachings of Jesus.

As I sat there thinking about what I had learned from the book, I suddenly had an urge to buy a bible so I could learn more about Jesus' life. It was approximately 2 am, and something in me said go and buy a bible. As faith would have it, there was a 24-hour bookstore just a few blocks away from where I lived, and it was one of my favorite hangouts.

When I got to the bookstore, I walked over to the religion section and started perusing through the different versions of the bible. I knew I didn't want to buy a King James Version because the language confused me. I found one called "The Student Bible," which is a New International Version of the bible written in plain English, which was definitely easier to read than the King James Version.

As I was walking home, I realized I had never purchased a bible before and had never really studied what was in it. What I really liked about this new bible was that it provided lots of additional commentary and insights about the Bible's stories, making it easier for me to understand the context in which the stories were written.

When I got home, it was approximately 3 am. For the first time in my life, I was actually excited about reading the bible and learning more about Jesus' life. Even though it was 3 in the morning, I decided to jump right in and start reading.

I knew from previous experience that the four gospels of the New Testament told the story of Jesus' life, so I immediately went to the chapter titled Matthew and began reading.

There is no way to put into words the miracle that occurred as I started reading, but I will do my best to try and explain what happened.

As I began reading, I felt as though I were transported back to the time Jesus walked the earth. I honestly felt as if I were there. As I continued reading, it was as if I was there with Jesus. As I got to the parts where Jesus was speaking, it felt as if he were sitting right next to me, teaching me his lessons. I had a highlighter marker, and I began highlighting his words and making notes of the insights I began to receive. As I continued to read his words, all of a sudden, it felt as if my heart opened up and I could feel the unconditional love of God moving through me. It was a feeling I cannot fully describe, but it felt like love multiplied by 1000. It was so powerful and intense that I began to cry with joy. As I continued to read, the feeling intensified, and I was enveloped by this unconditional love that came from inside of me and then wrapped itself around me like a blanket. In religious terms, I was bathed by the Holy Spirit; in spiritual terms, I was feeling the unconditional love of God.

For the next three hours, I continued to read and to feel this unconditional love. Tears of joy continued to flow as I absorbed the teachings of the Master. (I still have tearstains in that bible almost 30 years later. They are reminders of this miraculous magical experience that I will remember for the rest of my life.) When I got to the end of the chapter, I realized why I had never connected with God on such an intimate level. I had tried to find God in my head all of my life, but the truth was, it was always in my heart. I simply needed to be willing to let the love out that was already within me. Needless to say, this experience confirmed for me the presence of God, and it is why I have chosen to follow the teachings of Jesus and still consider him to be the greatest spiritual teacher who has ever walked this earth.

After that experience, I focused all of my attention on his teachings, and this book shares some of the lessons I have learned. And now, I would like to share a few of those lessons that have helped me create intimacy and connection to God that defies description and confirms for me the presence and the power of God.

Here are my ten favorite quotes from Jesus and my interpretation of what they mean.

1-Matthew 6:33 – Seek first the Kingdom of God and all else will be given to you.

Like most people, I used to believe that the kingdom of God was a place up in heaven with streets paved with gold and angels playing harps. But Jesus actually clarifies where the kingdom is in my next favorite quote.

2-Luke 17:20 – The kingdom of God does not come with your careful observation, nor will people say, Here it is, or There it is, because the kingdom of God is within you.

You can't get any clearer than that! The kingdom of God is within you! This quote from Jesus confirms what I've said throughout this book. There is a spark of divinity within you, and it is your responsibility to find it. It is truly amazing to me why most Christian religions do not accept this powerful truth. While most religions refer to Jesus as the source of miracles, the truth is that God's kingdom, or the spark of divinity, is actually the true source. Let me reiterate, the kingdom of God is within you. Put another way, there is a spark of divinity or a part of God that is within you. Jesus came to teach you how to access that part of yourself.

I find it interesting that Jesus said, "Seek first the kingdom," which I interpret as being the most important thing we must do. So, the next question we should be asking ourselves is this. "How do we enter into the kingdom?"

Once again, Jesus provides the answer with my favorite quote #3.

3-Matthew 18:3 – I tell you the truth, unless you change and become as little children, you will never enter the kingdom of heaven.

So, what exactly did he mean when he said, "you must become as little children?"

Take a moment and think about the qualities and attributes of a little child. Children are loving, forgiving, caring, nonjudgmental, accepting, playful, and curious. As we grow up, a lot of us lose these qualities. In doing so, we become close-minded, judgmental, skeptical, cynical, non-trusting, and unforgiving.

Jesus was saying that it is important for us to have what Buddhists call a "beginner's mind." The beginner's mind is open to new possibilities. It is just like a child's mind. It is inquisitive. It doesn't think it already knows everything; therefore, it is open to learning and having new experiences.

Becoming as little children is also a process of healing any childhood trauma you may be holding on to. As I mentioned in a previous chapter, I had to be willing to heal a lot of pain and trauma from my childhood to become emotionally free. Going to therapy, participating in workshops, and healing my heart from those traumatic experiences is what allowed me to "become as little children."

Therefore, becoming as little children is a literal and figurative comment. Jesus understood the power of healing, and he was directing us to do our inner work to heal our traumas and become emotionally and psychologically free.

This leads to my favorite quote #4.

4-Luke 9:12 – I tell you the truth, some who are standing here will not taste death before they see the kingdom of God.

I take this quote literally. You do not have to die before you enter the kingdom of God. From my own experience, I can say that I am already in heaven. As a result of the healing work I have done and the intimate connection I have with Divine Intelligence, I experience heaven every day.

Unfortunately, a lot of people may disagree with this, but I fervently believe that heaven on earth is possible. As a matter of fact, I believe it is inevitable. When every human being comes to an understanding and acceptance of the divine spark of God that is within them, this world will become heavenly.

This leads me to favorite quote #5

5-John 14:11 – Believe me when I say that I am in my father and the Father is within me; or at least believe on the evidence of the miracles themselves. I tell you the truth, anyone who has faith in me will do what I have been doing. He will do even greater things than these, because I am going to the Father.

Few people actually believe this quote. But by his own admission, Jesus says we can do the same things he did and even greater things. So what exactly did he do? The good book says he healed the sick, turned water into wine, made the blind see, raised someone from the dead, and overcame his own death. He went on to say that we could do even greater things than these. What if that's true?

Ultimately he started a movement that gave anyone who believed in him access to his father to do the things he did. So imagine what would happen if everyone followed his example? Don't you think this would be a beautiful world?

Here is favorite quote #6, which is a great follow up to quote #5.

6-Mark 11:24 Therefore I tell you, whatever you ask in prayer, believe that you have received it, and it will be yours.

Of all the quotes on this list, I think this is the most powerful one. Notice that Jesus says, "Whatever you ask in prayer." He put no qualifiers on that statement. He didn't say, whatever you ask for in prayer, as long as it isn't a million dollars. He didn't say, whatever you ask for in prayer, as long as it isn't a wonderful marriage. He didn't say, whatever you ask for in prayer, as long as it isn't healing an incurable disease. And he definitely didn't say, whatever you ask for in prayer, as long as it isn't world peace. He specifically said, "Whatever you ask for in prayer, believe that you have received it, and it will be yours."

So why would he say that?

I believe he said it because he knew nothing was impossible with God. He knew that believing in him would give us access to his Father, which is Divine Intelligence. So, do you believe him? Do you believe you can ask for anything in prayer and you will receive it?

I surely do!

Favorite quote #7

7-John 3:16 For God so loved the world that he gave his only begotten son, that whoever believes in him shall not perish but have eternal life.

This is definitely one of the most popular quotes from the bible. Most people would refer to Jesus as the son in this quote, but I interpret it a little differently. As I mentioned, I believe the actual son is Christ, the Divine Energy God released at the beginning of creation. Jesus was the personality through which God demonstrated the Christ, so it is the Christ which is eternal and provides everlasting life.

Favorite quote #8

8-John 4:23 Yet a time is coming and has now come when the true worshipers will worship the Father in spirit and truth, for they are the kind of worshipers the Father seeks. God is spirit, and his worshipers must worship in spirit and in truth.

Dr. Wayne Dyer stated, "You are not a human being having a spiritual experience, you are a spiritual being having a human experience." As a spiritual being, we are directly connected to God, which is spirit. By following Jesus' example, we can worship God in spirit and truth, and it gives us direct access to the unlimited power of God.

Favorite quote #9

9-Matthew 6:19 "Do not store up for yourself treasures on earth, where moth and rust destroy, and where thieves break in and steal. But store up for yourselves treasures in heaven, where moth and rust do not destroy, and where thieves do not break in and steal. For where your treasure is, there your heart will be also.

As human beings, we generally focus on things outside of ourselves for happiness. We think if we have the house, the wife, the 2.5 kids, the 401K, and the vacation, we will be happy. I definitely fell victim to this way of thinking early in my life. I have come to know that happiness is an inside job, and it does not take anything outside of ourselves to make us happy. This quote speaks directly to what it takes to be truly happy. Storing up treasures in heaven means we connect to our spiritual nature and recognize that connecting to Divine Intelligence is the source of true happiness. After we make that connection, then we can be truly happy with all the treasures of the earth.

Favorite quote #10

10-Matthew 22:37 "Love the Lord your God with all your heart and with all your soul and with all your mind and love your neighbor as yourself."

When Jesus was asked what the greatest commandment in the law was, this was his response. He knew that the most important relationship we could have was our relationship with God, and we should make sure that we loved God with all of our hearts. He then mentioned the importance of loving your neighbor as yourself, which if we truly loved God, we would also love our neighbor.

These are ten of my favorite quotes from Jesus that have made me genuinely happy with my life. I see each of these quotes as powerful life lessons from the world's greatest spiritual life coach.

If you learn these lessons for yourself and apply them to your own life, you can create the life of your dreams.

The bible isn't a book about how to get into heaven, it's a library of poems and letters and stories about bringing heaven to earth now, about this world becoming more and more the place it should be. There is very, very little about what happens when you die. That's not what the writers were focused on. Their interest, again and again, is how this world is arranged. Does everyone have enough? Are the power structures tilted in favor of the vulnerable? Has violence been renounced, or is it being kept in circulation?

Rob Bell
Everything Is Spiritual: Who We Are and What We're Doing Here.

CHAPTER 6
Revelations

Did you ever play a game in junior high school in which the teacher would whisper a story to the student in the front row of the class and then instruct that student to tell the same story to the person behind them? The goal was to share the story with every person in the class and then have the last person share the story they were told back to the class. Did you ever play that game?

If you've never played it, it's a fun game to play that teaches how people will change a story unintentionally based on their own interpretations of what they heard. It never fails; by the time the story gets to the last student, it is completely different from the original story.

Every religion works the same way. They are based on stories that were passed down for hundreds of years, and in a lot of cases, the stories were changed unintentionally based on the interpretations of the religious leaders of that time.

For example, think about Christianity. Christianity is based on the bible, yet according to Gordon-Conwell Theological Seminary, there exist roughly 43,000 Christian denominations worldwide in 2012. That is up from 500 in 1800 and 39,000 in 2008, and this number is expected to grow to 55,000 by 2025.

Think about that for a moment. There are 43,000 different Christian denominations, and they are all using the same bible filled with the same stories. So each denomination has its own interpretation of what the bible teaches, and their particular denomination believes that their interpretation is "the right" interpretation of the bible.

I believe that every major religion is simply a revelation from Divine Intelligence that is intended to inspire humanity to create heaven on earth. Therefore, all religions originate from the same source and lead to the same place. That place is oneness with the Divine, or put another way, oneness with God.

I'd like to share some insights I've learned about the five most popular revelations from Divine Intelligence and why I chose the bible as my primary source of spiritual inspiration and guidance.

I mentioned earlier there are approximately 4300 different religions in the world. The five primary and most popular ones are Christianity, Islam, Hinduism, Buddhism, and Judaism. The primary text of Christianity is the bible. For Islam, it's the Quran. For Hinduism, it's the Bhagavad Gita. For Judaism, it's the Torah, which are the first five books of the Old Testament in the bible. Although Buddhists do not consider Buddhism an actual religion, their teachings come from a collection of foundational texts called canons.

For easy reference, I'll simply refer to all of these revelations as spiritual texts. All spiritual texts are simply revelations from Divine Intelligence. The intention of all spiritual texts is to support human beings in recognizing their divinity and developing intimacy and connection to God.

Now take a moment and think about this. What do you think? Do you think there is only one path to God? Do you think each spiritual text comes from a different God? What do you truly believe? What is your truth? I mentioned earlier that my intention isn't to tell you what to think but to challenge you to think. So ask yourself honestly, what do you think?

I find it amusing that each religion teaches that their spiritual text is the "right" text and all others are wrong. This was one of the primary reasons I had such difficulty with organized religion. It simply did not make sense to me that a loving creator would choose one group of people to be his chosen people. As I understand it, all people are the chosen people because all people are simply divine expressions of God. Therefore, one religion is not the chosen religion or the right religion because all religions originate from the same source and lead to the same place. We are all children of God, and we choose different paths to get us back home to this understanding. This means every religion is the "right" religion if it leads you to intimacy and connection with God.

Once I began my journey to find my truth about God, there was one question I had to answer in order to come to terms with believing God existed. Why should I believe the bible? Whenever I asked a minister this question, they usually gave the same answer, "Because it was the word of God!" But that didn't sufficiently answer my question. How was I to know it was the word of God?

So I decided to find the answer to the question, "why should I believe the bible," and this is what I found.

First of all, I found out the bible is comprised of 66 different books which were written over several hundred years. They were based on stories that had been passed down for thousands of years. Originally, the bible was written in Hebrew, and then it was translated into Greek and eventually translated into English. As a result of the translations, a lot of the messages were misinterpreted, which is one of the reasons we have so many different religions based on the same stories from the bible.

After learning about some of the origins of the bible, I then began researching Jesus' life. I wanted to learn what he taught and how I could apply the things he taught to my own life. I started with the four Gospels of Matthew, Mark, Luke, and John, which begins the New Testament section of the bible. I started there because they were the chapters that told the stories of Jesus' life, and they are the only chapters in which Jesus actually speaks. I was surprised to learn that none of these books was actually written when he was alive. Most religious scholars believe Matthew was written 55 years after Jesus' death, Mark was written 50 years after his death, Luke was written 60 years after his death, and John was written 90 years after his death. It's actually unclear if the gospel writers actually met Jesus.

What convinced me of the Bible's authenticity was the feeling I got as I read the words of Jesus. There was something spiritual about his teachings that touched my soul.

As I deepened my understanding of Jesus' life, I came to the conclusion that there is a reason the bible is divided into the Old Testament and the New Testament. In the Old Testament, God was an angry, judgmental, and almost maniacal God. Here are a few scriptures that support this idea.

Deuteronomy 21:18 *"If someone has a stubborn and rebellious son who does not obey his father and mother and will not listen to them when they discipline him, ¹⁹ his father and mother shall take hold of him and bring him to the elders at the gate of his town. ²⁰ They shall say to the elders, "This son of ours is stubborn and rebellious. He will not obey us. He is a glutton and a drunkard." ²¹ Then all the men of his town are to stone him to death. You must purge the evil from among you. All Israel will hear of it and be afraid.*

Wouldn't this passage be hypocritical since one of the commandments God sent us was "Thou shall not kill?"

Since God commanded human beings not to kill, why would he resort to killing all of the firstborn sons of the people of Egypt because he was upset that the Pharoah would not release his people?

In Exodus 11:4-6 it says: *"This is what the LORD says: 'About midnight I will go throughout Egypt, 5 and every firstborn son in the land of Egypt will die, from the firstborn of Pharaoh who sits on his throne, to the firstborn of the servant girl behind the hand mill, as well as the firstborn of all the cattle. 6 Then a great cry will go out over all the land of Egypt. Such an outcry has never been heard before and will never be heard again...."*

Is that not the ultimate contradiction?

I definitely do not believe the bible was written to be taken literally. Unfortunately, a lot of religions interpret it that way. Based on these two scriptures alone, it insinuates that God is angry and judgmental.

Throughout the Old Testament, the stories imply that God had the same emotions like a normal human being, and most religions promoted that idea. Religions taught we were supposed to fear God and not make him angry; otherwise, he would punish us. And, of course, the ultimate punishment would be banishment to hell. Therefore, the Old Testament preached a fear-based theology.

In the New Testament, we are introduced to a love-based theology founded on the teachings of Jesus. Jesus came to teach us that God wasn't this angry, judgmental maniacal God. God was a God of love that loved us unconditionally, and he loved us so much that he sent his only begotten son to teach us how to access the unconditional love that he had given us access to.

I believe that the New Testament actually overrides the Old Testament, tells the truth about God, and provides us with a roadmap to bring us home to Divine Intelligence. Jesus' primary message is that God is love, and by following his teachings and example, we each have equal access to this love.

With this understanding, I have accepted that the bible is definitely the inspired word of God and the greatest revelation to man of God's existence. In no way does this imply that the bible is better than other revelations; it is simply my truth and the one that resonates the deepest in my heart.

With that being said, I enjoy reading spiritual texts from all of the major religions. Each one provides me with insights and inspiration to deepen my connection to Divine Intelligence.

I also believe that spiritual texts do not have to be hundreds of years old to come from God. As a matter of fact, countless people today are sharing insights and wisdom that supports us in deepening our connection to Divine Intelligence. You can call them messengers, influencers, spiritual gurus or spiritual teachers, but as long as their teachings help bring you closer to God, the name you use to describe them is irrelevant.

Here are a few of my favorite spiritual teachers who are alive today and sharing spiritual insights that encourage you to find your truth and connect with Divine Intelligence.

Neale Donald Walsch (www.nealedonaldwalsch.com)

Neale is the author of a series of books called Conversations With God. His writings have deeply influenced me, and his message is one of love and Unity for all humanity. While reading his books, I honestly feel as if God is speaking directly to me through Neale. His books confirm what I have always believed - God is Pure Love and is always speaking to everyone all the time. As he mentions in one of his books, "The question isn't to whom does God speak. The real question is how many of us are willing to listen when God speaks, because God speaks to everyone all of the time." I highly recommend any of his books, but I suggest you begin with Conversations With God Book 1 if you have not read any of his books. His latest book is called The God Solution, and it provides a unique blueprint for moving humanity forward by recognizing God as Pure Love. I highly recommend any of his books.

Gary Zukav

Gary wrote an amazing book called The Seat Of The Soul, which Oprah declared as one of her all-time favorites. It definitely falls into the same category for me, and his insights have inspired me to continually deepen my connection to Divine Intelligence. He also wrote a book titled The Dancing Wu Li Masters, which makes quantum physics accessible to everyone, and it will challenge your view on reality and how the Universe works. I recently completed his latest book titled Universal Human, and it filled me with hope and optimism about the future of humanity.

Barbara Marx Hubbard

Unfortunately, Barbara passed away on April 10th 2019, but she definitely left an indelible mark on my heart with her wisdom and compassion for humanity. In her book, Conscious Evolution, she theorized that human beings are still evolving and they are evolving to what she calls Homo-Universalis. This theory drew me to her work, and I loved engaging in programs she offered to help bring humanity together. She was such a bright light in the world, and her light continues to shine around the globe because of her teachings and philosophies.

Oriah Mountain Dreamer

Have you ever read something that touched you so deeply and inspired you so much that you wanted to meet the author to thank them for their inspirational words? This occurred for me back in 1999 when I was introduced to a poem called The Invitation by Oriah Mountain Dreamer. As I read the poem, it touched my heart in such a way that I knew it was a divine revelation I was supposed to be reading. This is what a true revelation does. It touches you and inspires you to feel the truth within its words, and it transforms you emotionally and spiritually. I was so moved by this poem that I located where the author was doing a book signing and flew from Houston, Texas, to New York just to meet her and thank her for writing such a powerful and heart-warming poem.

I was fortunate enough to meet her, and I had the opportunity to thank her for her beautiful poem, and she was just as beautiful inside and out as the poem she had written. This poem helped awaken me to my true purpose, and it inspired me to continue my spiritual journey to find the truth that set me free.

It is definitely one of my all-time favorite poems and revelations that inspired me along my spiritual journey.

The Invitation
By Oriah Mountain Dreamer

> It doesn't interest me what you do for a living. I want to know what you ache for and if you dare to dream of meeting your heart's longing.
>
> It doesn't interest me how old you are. I want to know if you will risk looking like a fool for love, for your dream, for the adventure of being alive.

It doesn't interest me what planets are squaring your moon. I want to know if you have touched the centre of your own sorrow, if you have been opened by life's betrayals or have become shrivelled and closed from fear of further pain.

I want to know if you can sit with pain, mine or your own, without moving to hide it, or fade it, or fix it.

I want to know if you can be with joy, mine or your own; if you can dance with wildness and let the ecstasy fill you to the tips of your fingers and toes without cautioning us to be careful, be realistic, remember the limitations of being human.

It doesn't interest me if the story you are telling me is true. I want to know if you can disappoint another to be true to yourself. If you can bear the accusation of betrayal and not betray your own soul. If you can be faithless and therefore trustworthy.

I want to know if you can see Beauty even when it is not pretty every day. And if you can source your own life from its presence.

I want to know if you can live with failure, yours and mine, and still stand at the edge of the lake and shout to the silver of the full moon, 'Yes.'

It doesn't interest me to know where you live or how much money you have. I want to know if you can get up after the night of grief and despair, weary and bruised to the bone and do what needs to be done to feed the children.

It doesn't interest me who you know or how you came to be here. I want to know if you will stand in the center of the fire with me and not shrink back.

It doesn't interest me where or what or with whom you have studied. I want to know what sustains you from the inside when all else falls away.

I want to know if you can be alone with yourself and if you truly like the company you keep in the empty moments.

Marianne Williamson.

One of the first spiritual books I read when I began my spiritual journey was A Return To Love by Marianne Williamson. It was a book that opened my heart and mind to the power of Love and how it was my responsibility to share my gifts and talents with the world to help make it a better place. Here is one of my all-time favorite poems she wrote, which was featured in her book.

Our Deepest Fear

Our deepest fear is not that we are inadequate.
Our deepest fear is that we are powerful beyond measure.
It is our light, not our darkness
That most frightens us.

We ask ourselves
Who am I to be brilliant, gorgeous, talented, fabulous?
Actually, who are you *not* to be?
You are a child of God.

Your playing small
Does not serve the world.
There's nothing enlightened about shrinking
So that other people won't feel insecure around you.

We are all meant to shine,
As children do.
We were born to make manifest
The glory of God that is within us.

It's not just in some of us;
It's in everyone.

And as we let our own light shine,
We unconsciously give other people permission to do the same.
As we're liberated from our own fear,
Our presence automatically liberates others.

I love the part where she says, "Your playing small does not serve the world." That quote inspired me to become a spiritual thought leader and begin writing books that expressed my deepest truths.

After watching her run for the presidency of the United States, it only deepened my admiration of her. Although I'll never run for political office, I will definitely follow in her footsteps by combining my spiritual beliefs with my political philosophy and using them both to positively impact the world.

These are just a few of the many spiritual teachers who have influenced my beliefs about God with their spiritual teachings, books, and lectures. They confirm that God is still providing humanity with revelations to help us deepen our connection and understanding of spiritual laws and how the Universe operates. But most importantly, they are teaching us that God is love and that all things are possible with love.

I hope this chapter has provided you with some fuel for contemplation about revelations from Divine Intelligence. My hope is that it will open your heart and mind to locate your own individual truth, and as you wake up to it, it inspires you to share your truth with others so that they too can find their own truth.

That's what we are here to do, so remember the words from Marianne Williamson,

"And as we let our own light shine,
We unconsciously give other people permission to do the same.
As we're liberated from our own fear,
Our presence automatically liberates others."

"There are only two ways to look at life. One, is as if nothing is a miracle, and two, is as if everything is a miracle."

- **Albert Einstein**

CHAPTER 7
Miracles

DICTIONARY DOT COM defines a miracle as *an effect or extraordinary event in the physical world that surpasses all known human or natural powers and is ascribed to a supernatural cause.* Put another way, a miracle could be defined as "A divine manifestation from Divine Intelligence that transcends human understanding."

One thing that definitely sets Jesus apart from other human beings was his ability to manifest miracles. What I find intriguing is the fact that not once throughout the bible did he take credit for any of the miracles he performed. In John 14:10, Jesus says: *[10] Don't you believe that I am in the Father, and that the Father is in me? The words I say to you I do not speak on my own authority. Rather, it is the Father, living in me, who is doing his work. [11] Believe me when I say that I am in the Father and the Father is in me; or at least believe on the evidence of the miracles themselves. [12] Very truly I tell you, whoever believes in me will do the works I have been doing, and they will do even greater things than these, because I am going to the Father. [13] And I will do whatever you ask in my name, so that the Father may be glorified in the Son. [14] You may ask me for anything in my name, and I will do it.*

This passage points to the idea that Divine Intelligence is the source of all miracles, and once we gain access to it, nothing is impossible. Jesus clearly recognized that his Father was the source, not him, but his job was to teach us how to connect with his Father so that we, too, could perform miracles. He knew that his job was to glorify the Father and lead by example so that others could do the same things he did.

In John 14:23, he stated, *"If anyone loves me, he will obey my teaching. My Father will love him, and we will come to him and make our home with him. He who does not love me will not obey my teaching."*

Put another way, if we love Jesus and follow his teachings, it will open our hearts to God and give us access to perform miracles.

I'd like to share ten of the miracles Jesus performed, which I copied from the website Christianity.com. This isn't a complete list of his miracles, but it definitely sets the context for this chapter.

1. Jesus changed water into wine (**John 2:1-11**).

On the third day, a wedding took place at Cana in Galilee. Jesus' mother was there, and Jesus and his disciples had also been invited to the wedding. When the wine was gone, Jesus' mother said to him, "They have no more wine." "Woman, why do you involve me?" Jesus replied. "My hour has not yet come." His mother said to the servants, "Do whatever he tells you." Nearby stood six stone water jars, the kind used by the Jews for ceremonial washing, each holding from twenty to thirty gallons. Jesus said to the servants, "Fill the jars with water," so they filled them to the brim. Then he told them, "Now draw some out and take it to the master of the banquet." They did so, and the master of the banquet tasted the water that had been turned into wine. He did not realize where it had come from, though the servants who had drawn the water knew. Then he called the bridegroom aside and said, "Everyone brings out the choice wine first and then the cheaper wine after the guests have had too much to drink; but you have saved the best till now." What Jesus did here in Cana of Galilee was the first of the signs through which he revealed his glory, and his disciples believed in him.

2. The great haul of fishes (**Luke 5:1-11**).

One day as Jesus was standing by the Lake of Gennesaret, the people were crowding around him and listening to the word of God. He saw at the water's edge two boats, left there by the fishermen, who were washing their nets. He got into one of the boats, the one belonging to Simon, and asked him to put out a little from shore. Then he sat down and taught the people from the boat. When he had finished speaking, he said to Simon, "Put out into deep water, and let down the nets for a catch." Simon answered, "Master, we've worked hard all night and haven't caught anything. But because you say so, I will let down the nets." When they had done so, they caught such a large number of fish that their nets began to break. So they signaled their partners in the other boat to come and help them, and they came and filled both boats so full that they began to sink. When Simon Peter saw this, he fell at Jesus' knees and said, "Go away from me, Lord; I am a sinful man!" For he and all his companions were astonished at the catch of fish they had taken, and so were James and John, the sons of Zebedee, Simon's partners. Then Jesus said to Simon, "Don't be afraid; from now on you will fish for people." So they pulled their boats up on shore, left everything and followed him.

3. Jesus cast out an unclean spirit (**Mark 1:23-28**).

Just then a man in their synagogue who was possessed by an impure spirit cried out, "What do you want with us, Jesus of Nazareth? Have you come to destroy us? I know who you are—the Holy One of God!" "Be quiet!" said Jesus sternly. "Come out of him!" The impure spirit shook the man violently and came out of him with a shriek. The people were all so amazed that they asked each other, "What is this? A new teaching—and with authority! He even gives orders to impure spirits and they obey him." News about him spread quickly over the whole region of Galilee.

*4. Jesus healed a leper (**Mark 1:40-45**).*

A man with leprosy came to him and begged him on his knees, "If you are willing, you can make me clean." Jesus was indignant. He reached out his hand and touched the man. "I am willing," he said. "Be clean!" Immediately the leprosy left him and he was cleansed. Jesus sent him away at once with a strong warning: "See that you don't tell this to anyone. But go, show yourself to the priest and offer the sacrifices that Moses commanded for your cleansing, as a testimony to them." Instead he went out and began to talk freely, spreading the news. As a result, Jesus could no longer enter a town openly but stayed outside in lonely places. Yet the people still came to him from everywhere.

*5. Jesus healed the centurion's servant (**Matthew 8:5-13**).*

When Jesus had entered Capernaum, a centurion came to him, asking for help. "Lord," he said, "my servant lies at home paralyzed, suffering terribly." Jesus said to him, "Shall I come and heal him?" The centurion replied, "Lord, I do not deserve to have you come under my roof. But just say the word, and my servant will be healed. For I myself am a man under authority, with soldiers under me. I tell this one, 'Go,' and he goes; and that one, 'Come,' and he comes. I say to my servant, 'Do this,' and he does it." When Jesus heard this, he was amazed and said to those following him, "Truly I tell you, I have not found anyone in Israel with such great faith. I say to you that many will come from the east and the west, and will take their places at the feast with Abraham, Isaac and Jacob in the kingdom of heaven. But the subjects of the kingdom will be thrown outside, into the darkness, where there will be weeping and gnashing of teeth." Then Jesus said to the centurion, "Go! Let it be done just as you believed it would." And his servant was healed at that moment.

*6. Jesus raised the widow)s son from the dead (**Luke 7:11-18**).*

Soon afterward, Jesus went to a town called Nain, and his disciples and a large crowd went along with him. As he approached the town gate, a dead person was being carried out—the only son of his mother, and she was a widow. And a large crowd from the town was with her. When the Lord saw her, his heart went out to her and he said, "Don't cry." Then he went up and touched the bier they were carrying him on, and the bearers stood still. He said, "Young man, I say to you, get up!" The dead man sat up and began to talk, and Jesus gave him back to his mother. They were all filled with awe and praised God. "A great prophet has appeared among us," they said. "God has come to help his people." This news about Jesus spread throughout Judea and the surrounding country. John's disciples told him about all these things.

7. Jesus stilled the storm (**Matthew 8:23-27**).

Then he got into the boat and his disciples followed him. Suddenly a furious storm came up on the lake, so that the waves swept over the boat. But Jesus was sleeping. The disciples went and woke him, saying, "Lord, save us! We're going to drown!" He replied, "You of little faith, why are you so afraid?" Then he got up and rebuked the winds and the waves, and it was completely calm. The men were amazed and asked, "What kind of man is this? Even the winds and the waves obey him!"

8. Jesus cured the paralytic (**Matthew 9:1-8**).

Jesus stepped into a boat, crossed over and came to his own town. Some men brought to him a paralyzed man, lying on a mat. When Jesus saw their faith, he said to the man, "Take heart, son; your sins are forgiven." At this, some of the teachers of the law said to themselves, "This fellow is blaspheming!" Knowing their thoughts, Jesus said, "Why do you entertain evil thoughts in your hearts? Which is easier: to say, 'Your sins are forgiven,' or to say, 'Get up and walk'? But I want you to know that the Son of Man has authority on earth to forgive sins." So he said to the paralyzed man, "Get up, take your mat and go home." Then the man got up and went home. When the crowd saw this, they were filled with awe; and they praised God, who had given such authority to man.

9. Jesus opened the eyes of two blind men (**Matthew 9:27-31**).

As Jesus went on from there, two blind men followed him, calling out, "Have mercy on us, Son of David!" 28 When he had gone indoors, the blind men came to him, and he asked them, "Do you believe that I am able to do this?" "Yes, Lord," they replied. 29 Then he touched their eyes and said, "According to your faith let it be done to you"; 30 and their sight was restored. Jesus warned them sternly, "See that no one knows about this." 31 But they went out and spread the news about him all over that region.

10. Jesus raised himself from the dead (John 14:28-31).

^{28} "You heard me say, 'I am going away and I am coming back to you.' If you loved me, you would be glad that I am going to the Father, for the Father is greater than I. ^{29} I have told you now before it happens, so that when it does happen you will believe. ^{30} I will not say much more to you, for the prince of this world is coming. He has no hold over me,^{31} but he comes so that the world may learn that I love the Father and do exactly what my Father has commanded me.

These are just ten of the many miracles Jesus performed and for most people they believe miracles were only performed two thousand years ago while Jesus was alive. But what about today in 2021? Are miracles still possible?

I believe the answer is an emphatic yes! So let's go back to what Jesus said in John 14:12-14?

^{12} Very truly I tell you, whoever believes in me will do the works I have been doing, and they will do even greater things than these, because I am going to the Father. ^{13} And I will do whatever you ask in my name, so that the Father may be glorified in the Son. ^{14} You may ask me for anything in my name, and I will do it.

Once again, I ask the question, why did he say that? Was this statement meant to be taken literally? For me, the answer is unequivocally, positively yes! Jesus healed the sick, made a crippled man walk again, foretold the future, made a blind man see again, manipulated the weather, and raised people from the dead. He even overcame his own death, and then he says, "These things and even greater things you shall do also," which says to me that we can do anything he did, and miracles are available to anyone who loves him and follows his teachings.

How and why is this possible? Because the true son of God is the Christ energy that is inherent in every human being. I mentioned in a previous chapter that Jesus was the personality that God used to express the Christ. So even though Jesus is no longer living, The Holy Spirit (Which is another name for the Christ Energy) is the divine spark of God in every human being, which gives us access to the Father, and with the Father, nothing is impossible. You can perform miracles in your own life by connecting with the Christ Energy, which is your connection to the Father/Creator.

To fully understand the science behind miracles, I'd like to introduce you to Dr. Joe Dispenza. (https://drjoedispenza.com) Dr. Dispenza was a chiropractor who broke his back in several places and was told that he would never walk again. However, he was able to heal his broken back without surgery by tapping into the Divine Intelligence within. Now he goes around the world teaching others how to access Divine Intelligence to heal their own bodies.

When science cannot explain the miracles of the human body, they use the term "spontaneous remission" to try and explain the unexplainable. Science does not use the term miracle, but I believe miracle is the correct term to use.

In Dr. Joe's case, he had this to say about his miraculous recovery. "*I believe that there's an intelligence, an invisible consciousness, within each of us that's the giver of life. It supports, maintains, protects, and heals us every moment. It creates almost 100 trillion specialized cells (starting from only 2), it keeps our hearts beating hundreds of thousands of times per day, and it can organize hundreds of thousands of chemical reactions in a single cell in every second—among many other amazing functions. I reasoned at the time that if this intelligence was real and if it willfully, mindfully, and lovingly had such amazing abilities, maybe I could take my attention off my external world and begin to go within and connect with it—developing a relationship with it."*

I believe the invisible consciousness he is talking about is the indwelling Christ. What is truly inspiring is how Dr. Joe teaches others how to heal their bodies using Divine Intelligence. There are countless confirmed cases of people from all around the world who have healed themselves from a wide variety of terminal illnesses and afflictions using his teachings and techniques. What is unique about his approach is how he uses science to explain and confirm how the body heals. He actually documents scientifically how and why the body can heal itself.

He is definitely a miracle worker who is teaching others how to perform miracles on their own by accessing Divine Intelligence.

When thinking about miracles, it's easy to focus on miracles concerning the human body and our physical health. Rest assured, countless other miracles are occurring every day. A miracle could be finding the perfect mate or landing the perfect job. It could be forgiving someone and rekindling a friendship. It could even be finding a large sum of money that you didn't expect. There are no limits to the miracles a person can receive, so simply be open to miracles and allow them to flow into your life.

To fully embrace miracles in your own life, you need to accept this one spiritual truth. There is but one presence and one power in the Universe: God, the good, omnipotent. I've mentioned that God is love. Therefore, the only thing this omnipotent power can do is love. This love is the source of all miracles. Thus, it is important to understand that everything that happens to us is done out of love.

With that being said, I'd like to share one of the greatest miracles that occurred in my life. At first, it may not sound like this is a miracle but rest assured it truly was.

One of my greatest miracles was my divorce!

I know what you're thinking. How can a divorce be a miracle? Let me explain.

I believe the Universe is perfect, and everything does happen for a reason. At the time of my divorce, I definitely didn't see it as a miracle.

My divorce was one of the most difficult and painful experiences of my life. It was so painful that I slipped into a deep state of depression and even considered taking my own life. But now, in retrospect, I can see how perfect my divorce was. I like to think of my divorce as a cosmic slap upside the head by Divine Intelligence. It knew that I was put on this earth to do extraordinary things, and it knew that I wasn't living up to my fullest potential.

I was trapped in an unhappy marriage that wasn't fulfilling or emotionally rewarding. I was stuck in a job with no room for advancement that didn't allow me to express my passions and creativity, and I was an Atheist who did not believe in a power greater than myself. So Divine Intelligence knew that it would have to take drastic measures to get my attention, and one way for it to do that was to interrupt my life to help me get on track. My divorce was that divine interruption I needed to wake me up. It was my miracle!

Because of my divorce, I went on this amazing journey to discover who I was and why I was put on this earth. As a result, I uncovered my unique gifts and talents of writing and speaking and fulfilled my lifelong dream of becoming an entrepreneur. If not for my divorce, I would still be trapped in an unhappy marriage with a woman I didn't love, and I would have still been trapped in a job working for someone else instead of being in control of my own destiny as an entrepreneur.

Can you now see the miracle of my divorce? Now take a moment and think about your own life right now. Is it possible that you are on the verge of receiving a miracle in your own life? Could it be that the current challenges you are experiencing are preparing you for something better? Is Divine Intelligence trying to tell you something? Are you willing to listen and trust it?

Here is another example of one of the many miracles I have received in my own life that confirms miracles are possible.

More than twenty years ago, I had a dream to run a company that would develop self-esteem building programs for children. I had no experience in developing programs, and I had no idea how to start a non-profit organization that would implement these programs. Despite my lack of knowledge and experience, I decided that I would start a company anyway. After several years of failure, I held on to my dream of building this company, but the reality was my life had actually fallen apart. I got to a point where I was homeless for a couple of years, and despite the challenges, I still held on to the dream.

Approximately seven years after I had conceived the idea for my company, I had no luck getting it funded. Despite this, I held on to my dream and continued to look for ways to bring my dream to reality. During this time, I was renting a rundown one-room apartment and making minimum wage working at a video store. I had a bicycle for transportation, and I could barely make ends meet. But somehow, I intuitively knew that I would eventually figure out a way to raise the money for my company.

One day while working at the video store, a man came in with his children and asked me if I could recommend some movies for them to watch. I made the recommendation, and he took them home to view them with his children.

A couple of days later, he came back and told me that his children absolutely loved the movies, and he wanted to thank me for the recommendations. He then became a regular customer that would always come in on the weekends and pick up movies to watch.

One evening, he came in and we started talking, and somehow we began talking about challenges in life. He then told me that he was dealing with a major challenge because he had recently been diagnosed with cancer. During our conversation, I mentioned some of the challenges I had gone through. I suggested to him that no matter how difficult challenges might be, there is always a positive lesson for us to learn within them.

When I said that, he smiled at me and said he completely agreed. He told me how his diagnosis had challenged him to really take a deep look at his life, and since he had been diagnosed, he had actually been happier with his life because, for the first time, he realized just how important his children were and how precious his life was. As a result of his cancer, he had become a better father and ultimately a better man.

After our conversation, we became close friends, and each time he

Chapter 7: Miracles

would visit, we would spend some time just chatting and supporting each other.

One day I was at work with a co-worker when my friend came in and asked for some movie recommendations. After he picked up his movies and left, my co-worker asked me if I knew who he was. I told him yes, and said that he was a friend of mine. My co-worker then asked me again, do you realize who that is? I said yes, his name is Mike and he is a good customer and a good friend of mine.

My co-worker then informed me that he was a very wealthy businessman who owned an oil company.

The next time my friend came to the store, I decided to ask him if he might be able to help me with my dream. I told him about my dream of creating the programs for kids, and I asked him if there was any way that he could help out. He then reached into his pocket and handed me one of his business cards. "Whatever you're working on, I would be glad to help you. Contact my secretary and make an appointment and let me see what I can do."

During this time, I was deeply involved with spiritual teachings and learned to keep my heart and mind open to miracles. I didn't know how he would help me, but I intuitively knew that somehow, he would.

I met him at his office a few days later, and I was pleasantly surprised to learn just how wealthy he was. His office was like something you would see on a television set. It was filled with sports memorabilia, wild animals, and pictures of my friend with former presidents and lots of celebrities.

I sat down and began explaining my idea to him. After I finished, he picked up the phone and contacted another wealthy businessman in charge of a non-profit foundation with access to lots of money. He told the person on the phone that I would be coming by to visit him and that he wanted to make sure that he would support my programs.

When he hung up the phone, he gave me another business card and told me to make an appointment to see the guy he had just spoken with, and he assured me that the man would be able to help me in some way. I thanked him repeatedly and let him know just how much

I appreciated his support. He then looked at me and said, *"I want to thank you for being my friend and for listening to me and sharing your dreams with me. I believe you are going to be very successful, and I am glad that I was able to help."*

A few weeks later, I met with the other businessman who loved my business idea, and several months later, I received a check for fifty thousand dollars to get my company started.

Let that sink in for a moment. I was completely broke, had no formal education or training, had a bicycle for transportation, and was living in a rundown dilapidated apartment that I could barely afford. Despite all of these challenges, I was able to receive a check for fifty thousand dollars! Do you think that was a miracle? I definitely do!

A lot of people would say that this was just a coincidence or I was just lucky. I, on the other hand, recognize that this had absolutely nothing to do with luck. It was divine synchronicity that orchestrated all of the events that led to me receiving the funding. It began with my belief that I would receive the funding. Faith is defined as evidence of things unseen, and I had unwavering faith that somehow, I would be able to secure funding. It was then followed by my willingness to work extremely hard to learn everything I needed to know about starting a nonprofit and keep my head above water while I was trying to start my company.

My faith and belief in Divine Intelligence and myself gave me the patience and persistence to not give up even after several years of failure. The key was my willingness to listen to my intuition and to trust that The Source would provide me with the guidance I needed to be at the right place at the right time to meet the right people. By relying on Divine Intelligence 100% and being willing to combine action with faith, I was able to locate the funding to get my company started.

This is why it is so important to learn to listen to and trust your intuition. As I've mentioned, Divine Intelligence is constantly communicating with us through our intuition. When we tune in and learn to connect the dots of synchronicity, The Source can guide us to our ultimate destiny.

So learn to listen to your heart and connect to your intuition, and you will receive all the guidance you need to create miracles in your life and create the life of your dreams.

I'd like to close this chapter with some ideas on how you can manifest miracles in your own life.

The first thing you have to do is be willing to enter the kingdom of God within your own mind. This means you must develop a connection to Divine Intelligence and learn to trust that it will guide you to miracles.

Next, you must "believe" that miracles happen. Have you ever noticed throughout Jesus' teachings that the only requirement he gave for manifesting miracles was to believe they were possible? Belief is the key that unlocks the door to all miracles. According to spiritual teacher Abraham Hicks, a belief is simply a thought that you think over and over again. If you accept the idea that thoughts are things, and what you think about you bring about, it's important for you to constantly think about the miracles you would like to manifest. Thinking is another form of praying. It is how you connect with Divine Intelligence. This is the reason prayer works.

It's important to recognize that prayer works as energy. It attracts to you that which you focus on. Therefore, if you're praying with positive thoughts, rest assured you will begin manifesting positive experiences. If you pray with negative thoughts, it stands to reason you will attract negative experiences.

Have you ever heard the saying, "Whatever the mind can conceive, you can achieve, if you truly believe?" This is a literal statement. If you combine that statement with this one, "The mind cannot distinguish the difference between what is real and what is vividly imagined," you have the recipe for manifesting miracles into your life.

Once you believe, the next thing you have to do is take action. In other words, you must pray then move your feet. Miracles do not necessarily appear out of thin air. You have to do something to help bring them to reality. For example, when I wanted to manifest the money to start my company, I didn't just sit there and pray and wait for something to happen. I took action! I wrote down my vision and put together a business plan to help me clarify my dream. I went to the library to learn about starting a business. I read lots and lots of books. I maintained a job to keep my head above water until I secured funding. I networked with others and made friends with people who ultimately helped me manifest the money. I took action, and you must too!

Was it easy? Absolutely not! But rest assured, it was definitely worth it!

Your next step is having patience and perseverance. It's important to know that God's delays usually aren't God's denials, so you must never give up or quit. Here is a great poem that illustrates the importance of perseverance. It's called; Don't Quit.

"When things go wrong, as they sometimes will,
When the road you're trudging seems all uphill,
When the funds are low and the debts are high,
And you want to smile, but you have to sigh,
When care is pressing you down a bit,
Rest, if you must, but don't you quit.

Life is queer with its twists and turns,
As every one of us sometimes learns,
And many a failure turns about,
When he might have won had he stuck it out;
Don't give up though the pace seems slow-
You may succeed with another blow.

Often the goal is nearer than,
It seems to a faint and faltering man,
Often the struggler has given up,
When he might have captured the victor's cup,
And he learned too late when the night slipped down,
How close he was to the golden crown.

Success is failure turned inside out-
The silver tint of the clouds of doubt,
And you never can tell how close you are,

It may be near when it seems so far,
So stick to the fight when you're hardest hit-
It's when things seem worst that you must not quit."

— John Greenleaf Whittier,

The final piece to manifesting miracles is having gratitude. When we learn to be grateful for everything that shows up in our lives, we set ourselves up to create a rewarding and fulfilling life. Gratitude is the energy that creates miracles. A grateful heart will always create more things to be grateful for. Gratitude is like a magnet for miracles. By being grateful and acknowledging Divine Intelligence, we attract everything we need to manifest miracles.

There you have it! The keys to manifesting miracles in your life.

1. Enter the kingdom of God through your mind.
2. Believe that miracles are possible.
3. Take action to manifest your miracles.
4. Give thanks to Divine Intelligence.

Now that you have those keys, I'll close this chapter with a powerful quote from Henry Ford. "Whether you believe you can, or believe you can't, you will always be right."

Believe you can manifest miracles, and you will!

"Imagination is more important than knowledge."

- **Albert Einstein**

CHAPTER 8
Ideas Are The Currency Of The Universe

I'D LIKE YOU to take a moment and think about the following items and see if you can recognize what they all have in common. An airplane, refrigerator, chair, book, cellphone, shirt, traffic light, sandwich, and a self-driving car. Do you have any idea what they all have in common?

Give up?

What they all have in common is they all began as a simple idea in someone's mind. If you think about anything that has ever been created on this planet, the fact remains it started as a single idea in someone's mind. Therefore, a crucial question you should be asking is, where did the idea come from?

Before I answer that question, let's go back to the early 1900s. Two brothers who owned a bicycle shop had an idea to create a machine that would allow people to fly. Can you imagine how crazy that idea must have sounded to everyone except the Wright brothers back then? Neither of the brothers had attended college, and they had no formal training in aeronautics. They had an idea to create something that had never been done before, and they had the faith, passion, and perseverance, to make their dream a reality. Their idea changed the world for the better, and they will always be remembered for the amazing contribution they made to humanity.

What about Henry Ford? Henry had an idea to create a horseless carriage. Despite the naysayers, he fulfilled his vision of creating the automobile and changed the course of history with his brilliant invention.

Dr. Martin Luther King Jr. had a unique idea that all people, regardless of race, should be accepted for the content of their character and not the color of their skin. His vision to bring equality to black people in America laid the foundation for the civil rights movement, which inspired this country to reexamine race relations and fulfil this country's creed that all men are created equal.

Possibly the greatest idea of all time came from Jesus. His idea was to grant access to his Father so that every human being would have access to their divinity through believing in him. His divine idea was, he was the son of God, and by accepting the idea, he was able to transcend his humanity and access his divinity, which he was willing to sacrifice so others could access their own.

After reading these four examples of people who had divine ideas that helped change the world, I circle back to my previous question, "Where did their ideas come from?"

Depending on who you ask, there are several different opinions about the answer to this question, but the answer will generally fall into three categories. Ideas are either psychological, anthropologic, or philosophical. Here are three ways to think about the origin of ideas I picked up on www.adgcreative.net

<u>Psychological</u> - For psychologists, ideas come from the brain, the mind. They're the product of synapses firing and connecting creative dots between thoughts and images and physical responses. The unconscious mind, where great ideas are thought to reside, also houses the bulk of our creative insights. Additionally, through the perspective of psychology, our own individual creativity grows exponentially when we're exposed to the creative ideas of others.

<u>Anthropologic</u> - Anthropologists, especially those of the social

and cultural variety, focus on how our surroundings shape and mold our thoughts and ideas. Innovation, prosperity, exchange – these are aspects of a communal society where members share their thoughts and bring ideas to life by working together instead of apart. The concept of diffusion is part of the anthropological perspective on ideas. How ideas spread from culture to culture is just as important as how they're created.

<u>Philosophical</u> - Philosophers, especially the likes of Descartes and Locke, believed ideas came from the soul. Objects and words caused ideas to form from intangible thoughts, and because of this, ideas were the mental representation of all things manifested in the brain. The philosophical perspective on ideas was that only human beings were capable of having them, that they were spontaneous and reflexive. All one had to do was simply breathe, and an idea would form.

I believe there are two answers to the question. Let me explain.

First of all, you need to understand the two aspects of who you are as a human being. I refer to these as the Big S Self and the Little S Self. Another way to put it is your Little S Self could be called your human self, and your Big S Self could be referred to as your Divine Self.

The Little S Self is connected to the brain. It processes everything based on memory and lived experiences. The Big S Self is connected to Divine Intelligence. It is the true source of all creative ideas. When the Wright Brothers had the idea to create an airplane, that idea originated from their Big S Self. When Jesus had the idea that he was the Son of God, that idea came from his Big S Self, or as he repeatedly stated, his Father in heaven. When it comes to the origin of where ideas come from, they either come from the Little S Self or the Big S Self.

As a human being, you have access to both. Unfortunately, very few people access their Big S Self. Jesus came to teach humanity how to access their Divine Self, which is connected to Divine Intelligence.

Since you're reading this book, I'm assuming you are open-minded and want to learn to access divine ideas for yourself, so I'd like to share some ideas for you to consider.

Remember the quote from Albert Einstein when he said,

"Everything is energy?" If you take the statement literally (which I believe you should), that means thoughts are energy. Therefore, everything you think creates an energetic vibration. Since we live in an energetic Universe, the thoughts you think send out a vibration, and the Universe will respond by sending back to you thoughts, feelings, and experiences that match the vibration you send out. This is called The Law Of Attraction. In biblical terms, this is what the quote from the bible "Do unto others, as you would have them do unto you," refers to. Some people call it Karma, and others refer to it as the law of cause and effect.

Since the overwhelming majority of people only pay attention to their Little S Self, they do not realize that their thoughts are creating their life experiences. In other words, what you think about you bring about.

Here's how it works.

Think about mainstream news. If you turn on the television, the overwhelming majority of stories you will see will be negative. Most people watch the news and then engage in conversations about what they watched. Have you ever had a conversation about something negative you've seen on television? Of course, you have. Everyone has. As people watch the negative news, it creates negative thoughts about the world. These negative thoughts create negative feelings, and these negative feelings send out a negative vibration which the Universe will respond to by sending back more negative thoughts, feelings, and experiences.

For example, one of the biggest news stories of 2021 was the January 6th attack on the US Capital by several supporters of the previous president Donald Trump. This story permeated the media for several weeks, and many people concluded that the US was headed for a civil war and our democracy had been destroyed. It also implied that race relations were getting worse in this country, and the country was definitely on the decline. As a result of the news story, there were record numbers of people buying bunkers and storm shelters to protect them from the upcoming collapse of America. Gun sales skyrocketed as people prepared themselves for the impending unrest.

Some of the people that were tuned in to those media broadcasts began having the thoughts that they needed to protect themselves. These thoughts of fear enticed them to do something to protect themselves. They then began speaking to friends and family about what was happening, and in some cases, they convinced friends and family members to believe what they believed. The Little S Self generated these thoughts. The Little S Self's job is to try and protect you from perceived threats. It does not matter if the threats are real or not, but if the Little S Self perceives them as such, its job is to try and protect you. I call these fear-based thoughts, and the Little S Self always generates them.

It does not matter what your opinion is of the event that took place. What matters is what thoughts do you have as a result of that event. Whatever your thoughts and beliefs are, the Universe will respond with corresponding thoughts, feelings, and experiences that match your thoughts. It is the universal law of cause and effect. Put another way, "As a man thinketh in his heart, so shall he be."

The point I am attempting to make is the importance of paying attention to what you are thinking. Thoughts are things and what you think about you bring about. You are what you think, and all of the experiences in your life are the result of what you have been thinking about the most. If you do not like what has been showing up in your life, then the first thing you must be willing to do is change the way you think.

My mentor, Dr. Wayne Dyer, put it this way, "If you change the way you look at things, the things you look at will change."

Let's take a look at some of the things you may be thinking about and see if you'd like to change the way you think about them.

Let's begin with how you see the world. Do you see a world that is falling apart or a world that is coming together?

What about love? Do you believe two people can create a lifelong love affair, or do you believe relationships are always filled with struggle?

What do you believe about your health? Do you think you have to be dependent on medication and that your health automatically declines as you age, or do you believe you can have dynamic health at any age?

How about money? Do you believe money is hard to come by and you always have to struggle to have enough of it, or do you believe there is plenty of money for everyone because we live in an infinite Universe?

And what about yourself? Do you love yourself? Do you see yourself as a divine child of the Universe with unlimited potential, or do you see yourself as unlovable and unworthy of love?

Be honest with yourself as you think about these questions.

Since my intention with this book is to inspire you and support you in becoming the best version of yourself by sharing wisdom from the Master Teacher Jesus, here is some fuel for contemplation for you to think about.

In his groundbreaking book, One Mind, Dr. Larry Dossey theorized there is one mind in the Universe, and all human beings are connected to this One Mind. This One Mind can be referred to as God, Divine Intelligence, Spirit, The Universe, or a host of other names, but his theory refers to it as One Mind.

Author and spiritual teacher Iyanla Vanzant said, "The mind is a powerful, creative energy. Everything we think, do and feel begins in the mind. For this reason, we have to address the thoughts, beliefs, judgments, learnings, and perceptions that we hold in our minds."

Both of these authors are making a distinction between the brain and the Mind. The brain is that mass of tissue inside your head that processes information and supports your bodily functions. The Mind is your connection to God. Some people believe that consciousness only resides within the brain, I on the other hand, disagree. The Mind is our connection to Divine Intelligence, and it extends beyond the mass of tissue inside your head. As Iyanla stated, it is a powerful creative energy.

Since the mind is a powerful creative energy, I would like to suggest something that may be a little difficult to swallow at first, but if you think about it, rest assured it will make a lot of sense by the end of this chapter.

Chapter 8: Ideas Are The Currency Of The Universe

As a human being, you are a Divine Idea in the Mind of God. To accept this idea, you must use your Big S Self or Divine Mind to grasp this concept. The Little S Self will not be able to accept this truth. I have mentioned several times throughout this book that you are Divine, and if you can wrap your mind around this idea, I will attempt to explain how this is possible.

Have you ever been deeply moved by something beautiful? Maybe it was a sunset or holding a newborn baby. Maybe it was a loving gaze by someone you cared deeply about. Or perhaps you were out in nature and experienced a deep sense of reverence and awe for the majesty of Mother Nature. Have you ever experienced the feeling of joy at such a deep level that it literally brought you to tears?

Have you ever pondered how a leatherback sea turtle that travels more than 12,000 miles between Indonesia and the United States knows how to return to the place of its birth to lay eggs and give birth to the next generation of turtles?

Or what about the great wildebeest migration in southeastern Africa, where more than 2 million wildebeest and 200,000 zebras and gazelle make an annual circular trip of more than 1,800 miles.

How do they know how to do that?

Or what about human sperm? How does it know to locate the egg and embed itself into it so that life can begin? And even more amazing, how does that simple act of impregnating the egg grow into this amazing thing called a human being?

How?

For me, the answer is simple. There is a Divine Energy and Intelligence that created and is still creating this amazing Universe. This intelligence is the source of all creation, and it is inherent in everything in the Universe. It is this Intelligence that drives animal migration and guides the sperm to find the egg. This intelligence is responsible for all of life and is the source of our feelings of love, beauty, joy, and awe. As the great Master Teacher Yoda put it, "For my ally is The Force, and a powerful ally it is. Life creates it, makes it grow. Its energy surrounds us and binds us. Luminous beings are we, not this crude matter. You must feel the Force around you; here, between you, me, the tree, the rock, everywhere, yes!"

As Master Yoda mentioned, "Luminous beings are we," and Divine Intelligence expresses itself through us, as us. Divine Intelligence communicates with us through Divine Ideas, and another word for Divine Ideas is imagination. Imagination is the "imaging in" of Divine Ideas. If you accept my theory that we are Divine Ideas in the mind of God, doesn't it make sense that God would communicate with us through ideas? I believe this is why Albert Einstein said, "Imagination is more important than knowledge." He intuitively knew the source of our imagination, and he recognized God as the source even though he didn't acknowledge this directly because of his scientific background.

If imagination is the imaging in of Divine Ideas, how does God get us to act on those ideas? I believe the answer is intuition. Intuition can be defined as; *"a natural ability or power that makes it possible to know something without any proof or evidence; a feeling that guides a person to act a certain way without fully understanding why."*

When we look at the animal kingdom, we describe this as instinct. Animals intuitively know what they are supposed to do. They don't have language to explain how they know; they simply know and that knowing or instinct guides them.

As human beings, we also have access to our instincts and intuition, but most people never access it. Why do you think that is? I believe the reason we don't is because we only pay attention to our Little S Self. Our Little S Self keeps us disconnected from our Big S Self, and until we connect with the Big S Self, we will never access our intuition and imagination.

Whether you realize it or not, you have access to your intuition, and you've used it possibly without even recognizing when you were using it. Ask yourself if you've experienced any of these situations.

You were thinking about someone when the phone rang, and it turned out to be the person you were thinking about.

You had a funny feeling in your gut that told you not to do

something, even though you wanted to, and then you listened to your gut, and it turned out to be right.

Something happened to you at just the right moment in a way that you didn't expect, but it helped you reach one of your goals.

You were thinking about a friend or someone you care about that you haven't seen in a while, and then you ran into them in a store or some unexpected place.

You were struggling with a problem, and suddenly, a solution popped into your head without you even thinking about it.

Has any of these things happened to you? I bet they have!

I'd like to share a story of how I used my imagination and intuition to rebuild my life and get my life back on track after my divorce.

I mentioned earlier that I became homeless after my divorce. During a brief period, I was living out of my car with no job or prospects, and I had no idea how I would be able to rebuild my life. Fortunately, I had been studying spiritual principles, and I began trusting that the Universe was perfect and everything that was happening to me was for my highest good. This was extremely difficult at times because sometimes I would go 2 or 3 days with nothing to eat, and I was sleeping in my car during the winter months and it would be extremely cold.

When I was living out of my car, I read a book titled Creative Visualization by Shakti Gawain. In the book, she talked about the power of visualization and why it was important to visualize the things you wanted to create in your life. After reading her book, I bought a pad of sticky notes, and I began writing down the things I wanted to create in my life. I would write down the things I wanted and then stick them to the back of my front seat so that I could see the notes as I lay down in the back seat.

After reading the book, the first thing I wrote on a note was I wanted to find a job. Finding a job was extremely difficult because I had a felony record for writing hot checks, and nobody would hire a felon. I was also a high school dropout which made it even more difficult to find a job. But I began visualizing myself finding a job. In the book, she talked about the importance of feeling the feelings

I would have once I received the job I was looking for. So I took her advice, and I would imagine how it would feel to finally have a job. I imagined myself finding a job and receiving a paycheck and eventually getting myself an apartment. I created the images in my mind and imagined how awesome it would feel to be back on my feet. I did all of this while sitting in the back seat of my car before I found a job.

After a few days of doing this, I looked through a local newspaper and saw an advertisement for laborers. I went to a place called the labor hall, and it was a place where homeless people, drug addicts, and ex-convicts went to find work. I was desperate for work, so I filled out a form and was told to sit and wait, and if something came up, they would call me up to go to the job. I sat there for six hours and was never called to work.

I went home a little disappointed, but I remembered what I had read in the book. Imagine the feelings you will have once you create what you want. So once again, I brought up the feelings of how good it was going to feel once I found a job and decided to go back again the next day. The next day, I sat there for eight hours and never got a job. That night while getting ready to go to sleep in my backseat, I said a little prayer. "God, I'm willing to do anything if you'll just give me a chance."

The next day, I went back to the labor hall and I was feeling pretty optimistic. I sat at the very front of the room and hoped I would be chosen to go for a job. After about an hour, the manager asked if anyone in the room had a car. I immediately raised my hand, and he called me to the window. "You have a vehicle?" Yes sir, I do. "Do you have gas?" How much do I need? "This job is about 30 miles away. Can you make it there and back?" I think so. "I tell you what, I'm not supposed to do this but I'm going to give you 10 dollars for gas money, but you will have to pay me back once you complete the job and get your check. Is that a deal?" Absolutely!

He gave me the address and told me to get there as soon as I could. As I was driving to the job, I had this huge smile on my face, and I was filled with joy. I was happy to have a job even though I had no idea

Chapter 8: Ideas Are The Currency Of The Universe

what I would be doing. I immediately thanked God for opening the door for me, and I counted my blessings all the way there.

Went I got to the job, my happiness immediately disappeared. It was a company that manufactured portable toilets, and I had an awful feeling that I was going to be cleaning them.

When I located the manager, he was one of the rudest, foulest, mean-spirited persons I've ever met. Every other word he used was a cuss word, and he treated me like I was a worthless piece of you know what. But since I was so happy to have the job, I looked past his attitude and simply wanted to do my job.

He took me out to the porta-potties, and as I suspected, my job was to clean them out. I had this huge vacuum cleaner type device that sucked out the feces and urine, and once I sucked that out, I had to scrub them down with a brush and disinfectant. It was disgusting!

After about an hour, it began to rain. Actually, it was more like a torrential downpour. I ran inside to see if I could wait until the rain stopped, but Mr. Knucklehead boss screamed at me to get a raincoat and go back out there and finish the job.

My first thought was to tell him to kiss my, you know what, and leave, but then I remembered my prayer to God. I said I was willing to do anything if I could just get a job, and even though I hated what I had to do, my prayers had been answered.

All of a sudden, my attitude completely changed. I felt a deep sense of gratitude, and I began thanking God for the job. I cleaned those toilets with a smile for eight full hours, and by the time I was finished, Mr. Knucklehead even complimented me for a job well done.

As I was driving back to the labor hall, my joy came back. I was grateful for completing the awful job with a smile, but most importantly, I was grateful that God had answered my prayers.

When I got back to the labor hall, I received my check, cashed it, repaid my ten-dollar debt and bought myself a delicious hamburger to celebrate. As I sat in the backseat of my car that night, I was filled with gratitude. I wrote a few notes of gratitude on some sticky notes and went to sleep.

The next day, as soon as I walked into the labor hall, the manager called me up front with a job. I immediately thanked God for the opportunity, and I was willing to do anything. This time it was the complete opposite of my previous experience.

The job was working with an electrical company that was working in a new office building. When I met the manager, he was extremely friendly and cordial. He took me around and introduced me to some of the electricians I would be working with, and each of them was also friendly and cordial. My job was to clean up and help the electricians with anything they needed.

One of the electricians and I started talking about my past jobs, and I told him how I used to manage a building supply center. He asked me if I knew anything about working with electrical tools, and I told him I was very familiar with them. We also talked about football and our children, and by the end of the day, we had become friends.

After the day was over, my electrician friend told me to meet him in the main office where the supervisor was. He told his supervisor what a great job I had done and convinced him to hire me full-time as his assistant. I went from making 5.75 per hour from the labor hall to 18.75 per hour working full time for the electrical company.

After approximately six weeks, I was able to save up enough money to get an apartment, and that was how I was able to use my imagination to get back on my feet.

There are several lessons you should take away from my story.

First of all, it is important to use your imagination to create whatever you want. It begins by making mental pictures in your mind of what you want to create. Remember, imagination is the imaging in of God's divine ideas. I started by imagining myself getting the job, and I wrote it down. It is imperative that you write down your vision of what you want because it tells the Universe you are serious. Once you write it down and begin visualizing what you want, you must bring up the feeling you will have as if you already have what you want. This is where faith comes in.

Once you have the vision, you must be willing to do whatever it takes to bring your vision to fruition. That means you have to pray and then move your feet. You must be willing to take action on your dream. Without action, your dream can't come true. Will it be easy? Probably not, but rest assured you have everything you need inside of you to move past any obstacle or challenge.

An essential part of this equation is gratitude. Having an attitude of gratitude will provide you with the emotional energy to move through all obstacles. Knowing Divine Intelligence is always working in your favor and everything is always in divine order gives you the faith and the feeling that anything is possible. So be sure and count your blessings no matter what situation you may be in.

Did you recognize how ideas were the key to me overcoming the challenges in my life? First, I had the idea to find a job. Next, I had the idea to look in the paper. Then I had the idea to go to the labor hall. Then I had the idea to say a prayer. And finally, I had the idea to thank God for providing me with the job that allowed me to begin rebuilding my life. All of these ideas came from my Big S Self. And by trusting my intuition to guide me, I was able to get back on track.

If I had not listened to my Big S Self, I could have easily fallen victim to depression, addiction, and hopelessness. I could have wallowed in self-pity and possibly turned to drugs or alcohol. By believing in a power greater than myself and then taking the necessary steps to do whatever it took to get my life back on track, I was able to overcome all of the adversities in my life. My story should inspire you to recognize that you have access to the same Divine Intelligence that supported me during those dark periods of my life. There is a spark of divinity within, and it is your responsibility to tap into it.

Once you develop intimacy and connection to Divine Intelligence, your life will become miraculous. You will begin to see how amazing life can be, and you will be able to see how every adversity and challenge actually brings you a gift and lesson that is intended to help you move closer to God.

I mentioned earlier that you are a divine idea in the mind of God, and when you fully understand and embrace this idea, you will get to a point where you recognize exactly what you showed up on this earth to do. It is called your divine purpose, and I believe every human being has one. The way to find your purpose is remembering what Jesus said, "Seek ye first the kingdom of heaven, and all things will be given unto you." Finding the kingdom is another way of saying connecting to your Big S Self. When you connect to your Big S Self, you will discover the unique gifts and talents you are born with. When you use those gifts and talents to help make the world a better place, you will have found your divine purpose.

Your divine purpose will always be found at the intersection of what you love to do and are good at, and that which the world needs. When you figure out these two things, then you will be on track to fulfill your divine purpose.

So how will you know when you are doing what you love? Here are three clues to let you know.

1-*If you are doing what you love, you will do it without thought of compensation.* This does not mean you can't make money doing it; it means you love doing it so much you really do not care if you make any money. You do it for the pure joy of doing it, and it feels good to do it.

2-*When you are doing what you love, time literally disappears.* Everyone has had experiences in which time literally flies by. As a writer, I can sit at my computer for eight hours writing, and it seems as if ten minutes have gone by. This is what happens when you do what you love.

3-*When you do what you love, you'll want to share it with others.* There is a joy that comes from sharing what you love with other people. When you put your heart and soul into something and then watch other people smile or enjoy what you've done, it will make you love what you do even more.

Now think about something you love doing and see if these three things hold true. If they do, you may have found what you love to do. But here is a word of caution. If you love doing something, but you're really not good at it, rest assured you have not found your purpose. When you find your purpose, you will love it, and you will be good at it.

It's now up to you to listen to ideas from Divine Intelligence to guide you to finding your purpose. Remember, God is always just a thought away, and when you learn to listen and trust it, it will guide you to your ultimate destiny.

Good luck!

Love Comes from God

Beloved, let us love one another, because love comes from God. Everyone who loves has been born of God and knows God. Whoever does not love does not know God, because God is love.

This is how God's love was revealed among us: God sent His one and only Son into the world, so that we might live through Him. And love consists in this: not that we loved God, but that He loved us and sent His Son as the atoning sacrifice for our sins.

Beloved, if God so loved us, we also ought to love one another. No one has ever seen God; but if we love one another, God remains in us, and His love is perfected in us. By this we know that we remain in Him, and He in us: He has given us of His Spirit. And we have seen and testify that the Father has sent His Son to be the Savior of the world.

Berean Study Bible John 1:4

CHAPTER 9
Sin And Punishment

IF I HAD to choose one thing that caused me to become an Atheist, it would have to be the biblical teachings of sin and punishment. Even as a child, I could not wrap my mind around the idea that a loving God would need to punish his creations. Why would God banish the children he supposedly loved to an eternal hell of fire? What would be the point? To me, this was the greatest contradiction of organized religion.

In John 4:16, it says, *"And so we know and rely on the love God has for us. God is love. Whoever lives in love lives in God, and God in them."* It says, "God is Love," so what kind of love would banish its children to eternal damnation? Is that love?

This was the contradiction that caused me to become an Atheist. I simply could not believe that a loving God would be so angry and vengeful that he would have to punish his children because they didn't follow his rules.

As mentioned in previous chapters, I took it upon myself to find the answers to all of my questions about God as a child. I was able to find my "truths" about God, and as I've done in previous chapters, I'd like to share some things I have learned which have allowed me to come to an understanding about God that puts my mind and my heart at rest in the knowing that God is real.

The most erroneous teaching I believe all organized religions adhere to is the idea that God is a "who", not a "what." Put another way, religions were built on the idea that God was made in man's image, not the other way around. Even though the bible says man was made in God's image, religions have projected human traits and attributes onto God and perpetuated this idea that God acts like human beings. There is overwhelming evidence of this in the Old Testament. In the Old Testament, God is portrayed as this tyrannical, judgmental, and angry God that gets his feelings hurt if someone disagrees with him or disobeys his orders. In Exodus 20:4, it even quotes God as saying, "I am a jealous God."

The bible teaches that God laid down a set of rules, and if people didn't follow those rules, he would get pissed off and then punish anyone who didn't follow them.

Here is a good example. As the creator of all things, God came up with the perfect way to propagate the species. He gave human beings the act of sex. Sex is possibly the most pleasurable experience a human being can have. This is by design. It is how God ensures that the species will survive and thrive. In Genesis 1:28, God says, "And God blessed them. And God said to them, 'Be fruitful and multiply and fill the earth and subdue it, and have dominion over the fish of the sea and over the birds of the heavens and over every living thing that moves on the earth.'"

God gives human beings this amazing gift called sex and tells them to use it to multiply the number of people on earth. Then religion steps in and adds restrictions and commandments that prohibits human beings from enjoying something God created. Let's look at a few scriptures that make my point.

2 Corinthians 12:21

"I am afraid that when I come again my God will humble me before you, and I will be grieved over many who have sinned earlier and have not repented of the impurity, sexual sin and debauchery in which they have indulged."

Ephesians 5:33

"But among you there must not be even a hint of sexual immorality, or of any kind of impurity, or of greed, because these are improper for God's holy people."

Galatians 5:19

The acts of the flesh are obvious: sexual immorality, impurity and debauchery;

1 Corinthians 6:9

Or do you not know that wrongdoers will not inherit the kingdom of God? Do not be deceived: Neither the sexually immoral nor idolaters nor adulterers nor men who have sex with men.

Once again, God gives man this amazing gift called sex and then religion convinces people that sex is bad, sex is a sin, and sex is only allowed during marriage and only between people of the opposite sex. God did not create these restrictions, men did. Religions created their own interpretations of how they believed God would view the act of sex. Their interpretations were based on the idea that God was a human being that would have judgments and opinions on how human beings behaved. Therein lies the real problem. Religion sees God as a human being with human emotions instead of seeing God as the Divine Energy and Intelligence that created and is still creating this amazing Universe that we live in.

Here is how I see things.

First of all, it's important to understand why there is an old and a New Testament. The Old Testament shares a metaphysical and metaphorical story about the origins of the Universe and how God operates. In the Old Testament, man was given ten commandments they were supposed to follow in order to remain in the good graces of God. Here are those commandments in case you've forgotten them.

1. "I am the Lord thy God, thou shalt not have any gods before Me."

This commandment forbids *idolatry*, the worship of false gods and goddesses, and it prohibits *polytheism*, the belief in many gods, insisting instead on *monotheism,* the belief in one God. This commandment forbids making golden calves, building temples to Isis, and worshipping statues of Caesar, for example.

2. "Thou shalt not take the name of the Lord thy God in vain."

The faithful are required to honor the name of God. It makes sense that if you're to love God with all your heart, soul, mind, and strength, then you're naturally to respect the name of God with equal passion and vigor.

3. "Remember to keep holy the Sabbath day."

The Jewish celebration of Sabbath *(Shabbat)* begins at sundown on Friday evening and lasts until sundown on Saturday. Catholic, Protestant, and Orthodox Christians go to church on Sunday, treating it as the Lord's Day instead of Saturday to honor the day Christ rose from the dead.

4. "Honor thy father and mother."

This commandment obliges the faithful to show respect for their parents — as children *and* adults. Children must obey their parents, and adults must respect and see to the care of their parents when they become old and infirm.

5. "Thou shalt not kill."

The better translation from Hebrew would be "Thou shalt not murder" — a subtle distinction but an important one to the Church. Killing an innocent person is considered murder. Killing an unjust aggressor to preserve your own life is still killing, but it isn't considered murder or immoral.

6. "Thou shalt not commit adultery."

The sixth and ninth commandments honor human sexuality. This commandment forbids the actual, physical act of having immoral sexual activity, specifically adultery, which is sex with someone else's spouse or a spouse cheating on their partner. This commandment also includes *fornication,* which is sex between unmarried people, prostitution, pornography, homosexual activity, masturbation, group sex, rape, incest, pedophilia, bestiality, and necrophilia.

7. "Thou shalt not steal."

The seventh and tenth commandments focus on respecting and honoring the possessions of others. This commandment forbids the act of taking someone else's property. The Catholic Church believes that this commandment also denounces cheating people of their money or property, depriving workers of their just wage, or not giving employers a full day's work for a full day's pay. Embezzlement, fraud, tax evasion, and vandalism are all considered extensions of violations of the Seventh Commandment.

8. "Thou shalt not bear false witness against thy neighbor."

The Eighth Commandment condemns lying. Because God is regarded as the author of all truth, the Church believes that humans are obligated to honor the truth. The most obvious way to fulfill this commandment is not to *lie* — intentionally deceive another by speaking a falsehood. So a good Catholic is who you want to buy a used car from.

9. "Thou shalt not covet thy neighbor's wife."

The Ninth Commandment forbids the intentional desire and longing for immoral sexuality. To sin in the heart, Jesus says, is to lust after a woman or a man in your heart with the desire and will to have immoral sex with them. Just as human life is a gift from

God and needs to be respected, defended, and protected, so, too, is human sexuality. Catholicism regards human sexuality as a divine gift, so it's considered sacred in the proper context: marriage.

10. "Thou shalt not covet thy neighbor's goods."

The Tenth Commandment forbids the wanting or taking of someone else's property. Along with the Seventh Commandment, this commandment condemns theft and the feelings of envy, greed, and jealousy in reaction to what other people have.

I have absolutely no problems with these commandments, and on the surface, they appear to be commandments that benefit humanity. But think about this, why would a loving God command us to do anything? A commandment wouldn't come from love. A commandment would only come from the mind of man, and all religions are the result of men interpreting what they believe to be God's word.

Since I believe God is the Divine Energy and Intelligence that created the Universe, I do not see these as commandments but as divine wisdom shared by a loving Creator to assist human beings in expressing the unconditional love of God. By embracing this wisdom and following God's guidance, we can create unified humanity that accepts one another for the unique expressions of God that we all are. If we choose not to follow this wisdom, we will not be condemned, punished, or rejected; we will simply miss out on the joy and passion that comes from following in God's footsteps.

The Old Testament laid the foundation for humanity to grasp the idea of a Creator, but unfortunately, it is based on the idea that God was a "who," not a "what."

On the other hand, the New Testament overrides the Old Testament and introduces us to the truth. God is spirit, and the true worshippers must worship in spirit and truth. Jesus showed up to demonstrate the unconditional love of God. Everything he taught expresses that unconditional love.

My invitation to you is to embrace the idea of this unconditional

Chapter 9: Sin And Punishment

love and recognize that you were not born a sinner, and no matter what you may have done, God does not judge or condemn you.

Do you know the origin of the word sin? Sin is actually a term used in archery, which means to miss the mark. When an archer shoots an arrow and completely misses the target, it is called a sin. Religion misinterpreted it as an act against God, which I believe is an erroneous teaching that has caused unnecessary pain and suffering in too many people's lives. Therefore, sin is not something that should be condemned, it is something that should be corrected.

It truly amazes me how so many people readily accept this idea of sin and punishment. Religion has convinced people to believe they were born sinners even though the bible specifically says we were born in the image and after the likeness of God. It also says explicitly that God is love, so therefore, we are born as perfect expressions of love, not sinners.

If you embrace the idea that God is the divine energy and intelligence that created and is still creating this amazing Universe we live in, instead of this angry anthropomorphic being who wants to punish us, the word sin takes on a whole new meaning. When we sin from this perspective, it simply means we are temporarily disconnected from God, and our job is to reconnect to God.

I'd like you to take a moment and think of something you may have done that you may have considered sinful. I don't care how "bad" you may think it was; simply bring the thought to mind. As you think about it, see if you can connect to the feelings you had when you did it. Did you feel positive emotions or negative emotions? Chances are, you probably felt negative emotions. Emotions like anger, guilt, shame, regret, and remorse. It's important to accept that emotions are neither good nor bad, they are simply energy in motion. Therefore, the energy is either positive or negative, not good or bad. This is a very important distinction you must make.

As you think about what you did, how do you feel right now? Do you still feel those negative emotions? If you accept the religious teachings that you sinned, I'm certain you will feel negative emotions. On the other hand, if you accept that sin is something to be corrected, you now have the opportunity to correct or make amends for whatever you did, and in doing so, you will begin to feel a positive energy. This is where forgiveness comes in, and it was one of the most powerful lessons Jesus taught us.

In Luke 23:34, Jesus was being crucified and nailed to the cross when he cried out, "Father forgive them for they know not what they do." Even though his captors were committing the ultimate sin of murder, Jesus recognized the perfection of his life's purpose, and he understood God's plan for his life. He intuitively knew that his Father would fulfill his promise of raising him from the dead, so therefore, he did not judge nor condemn the actions of his persecutors. This was the ultimate act of forgiveness, and it teaches us the importance of forgiveness.

With that being said, you need to be able to forgive yourself for any "sin" you may have committed. Remember, sin is something to be corrected, not condemned. So what do you need to correct or make amends for so you can let go of any negative feelings you may have been carrying around?

I'd like to share a story from my own life about the power of forgiveness.

After my divorce, I was in deep financial trouble. I was trying to maintain two households because my former wife did not have a job. Additionally, the economy had taken a nosedive. And since my job was based on commission, I had experienced a 30% decrease in my income because of the recession.

In an attempt to keep my head above water, I wrote several bad checks to try and cover my expenses. Each time I wrote a bad check knowing that I didn't have the money in the bank, I was filled with guilt and shame. The guilt and shame were so unbearable that I spiraled into a deep state of depression. I felt like such a failure, but I couldn't figure out anything else to do at the time.

Eventually, it all caught up to me, and the company I worked for found out about the checks. They filed theft by check charges against me, and obviously, I lost my job. Things went from bad to worst.

The good news is, this experience caused me so much emotional pain that I had to do something to alleviate it, so I gained the courage to go to therapy, and I began the process of my healing and transformation. One of the things I learned in therapy was the importance of forgiving myself for the mistakes I had made. I blamed myself for being a bad husband, a bad father, and an overall bad man, but my therapist helped me see that I wasn't a bad man and I was actually a good husband and a great father. With her guidance, I was able to forgive myself for the mistakes I had made, and I was able to release all of the shame and guilt I had been carrying around for a very long time.

Healing the shame and guilt I felt was a process that was difficult and painful. Still, as a result, I no longer felt like a failure, and I eventually got to a place of learning to love and accept myself unconditionally. This was confirmed when I was arrested for the bad checks I had written. I remember when the officer came by my apartment to arrest me, and he handcuffed me and put me in the backseat of the police car. As I sat in the backseat, I remember feeling calm and at peace, and there was absolutely no shame whatsoever. When we got to the courthouse, I was escorted through the building, and I was smiling the entire time. I was smiling because I recognized that I had made some mistakes and had to accept the consequences of my choices, but although I had made some poor choices, I was still a good man, and there was nothing for me to be ashamed of. Words cannot describe how good it felt at the time not to be ashamed of the mistakes I had made.

When I met with the judge, I took full responsibility for what I had done. I apologized for my actions and told him I would accept whatever punishment he felt I deserved. Since I didn't have any prior offences, I was sentenced to probation and community service and did not have to do any time in jail.

As I left the courthouse, I was filled with joy and excitement. I had learned some very valuable lessons, and the most important one was, I was a man who made some poor choices, and that did not make me a bad man. I had learned to forgive myself for the choices I had made, and in addition, I had learned to love myself and accept myself for the wonderful person I've always been. Self-love and self-acceptance were the reasons I felt the joy and excitement.

Now bring your attention back to something you may have done that you considered "sinful." After reading my story, can you now see that your mistake is something to correct, not condemn? You did not sin. You simply made a choice, and you have to accept the consequences of that choice. Remember, God does not, and cannot punish you for the choices you have made. God can only do one thing, and that one thing is love. If you are experiencing any negative feelings or experiences because of the choice you made, it is your responsibility to take full ownership for what you have done and learn to forgive yourself and let go of any negative emotions you may be holding on to. This does not condone what you have done; it allows you to make amends and let go of any negative feelings you may have about yourself because of what you did. The key is to release any negative thoughts, feelings or beliefs you may be holding on to because of what you've done. This is why forgiveness is so important. It allows you to be free of that negative energy.

You need to understand that as human beings, we always make the best possible choice for ourselves in that moment based on our limited amount of understanding. In other words, if we knew better, we would have done better. If we do not like the consequences of our choices, we must be willing to make better choices. To do so, we must increase our understanding. This is the reason you should read books like this to help you increase your understanding so you can make better choices in your life.

Your take away from this should be, you are not a sinner, and a sin is something to be corrected, not condemned. You must recognize we all make mistakes, and even when we do, God loves us because love is what God is. God does not punish or condemn; it simply expresses the love that it is. If we don't feel that love, it is because of something we have done, not something God has done.

This brings us to another topic. Heaven and hell.

Do you believe in either of them?

Growing up, I imagined angels with harps and streets paved with gold, and a fiery furnace with a red devil and horns. What about you? What were you taught about heaven and hell? Did you believe what you were taught?

Here is what I believe in regards to heaven and hell.

First of all, I do not believe they are geographical places. In other words, there isn't a physical heaven above us in the clouds, nor a physical hell below us deep within the earth. I believe heaven and hell are actually states of consciousness which we experience in our minds and hearts.

Do you remember the quote from Luke 17:21 in the bible, which says, "The kingdom of God is within you?" If you will accept my definition of God, which is, "the divine energy and intelligence that created and is still creating the Universe," then it stands to reason that our connection to this intelligence is our minds. That is why it says the kingdom of God is within you. The only way to enter the kingdom is through our minds and our hearts. In other words, through our thoughts and feelings.

When our thoughts and feelings are in alignment with Divine Intelligence, we reside in heaven. When our thoughts and feelings are out of alignment with Divine Intelligence, we then reside in hell. So the way to distinguish if you are in heaven or hell is to pay attention to your feelings. Your feelings are the language of your soul, and they are the feedback mechanisms of your heart. When you are feeling positive emotions like love, optimism, joy, and hope, you are in a state of heaven. When you are feeling negative emotions like hate, anger, resentment, and fear, you are in a state of hell.

The truth is, you have complete control over whether or not you are in heaven or hell. It is always your choice. God does not choose where you are, you do. To help you understand this, I'd like to share something I learned from a guy named David Hawkins. David wrote a remarkable book titled Power Versus Force. In the book, he created something he calls a Map of Consciousness Scale.

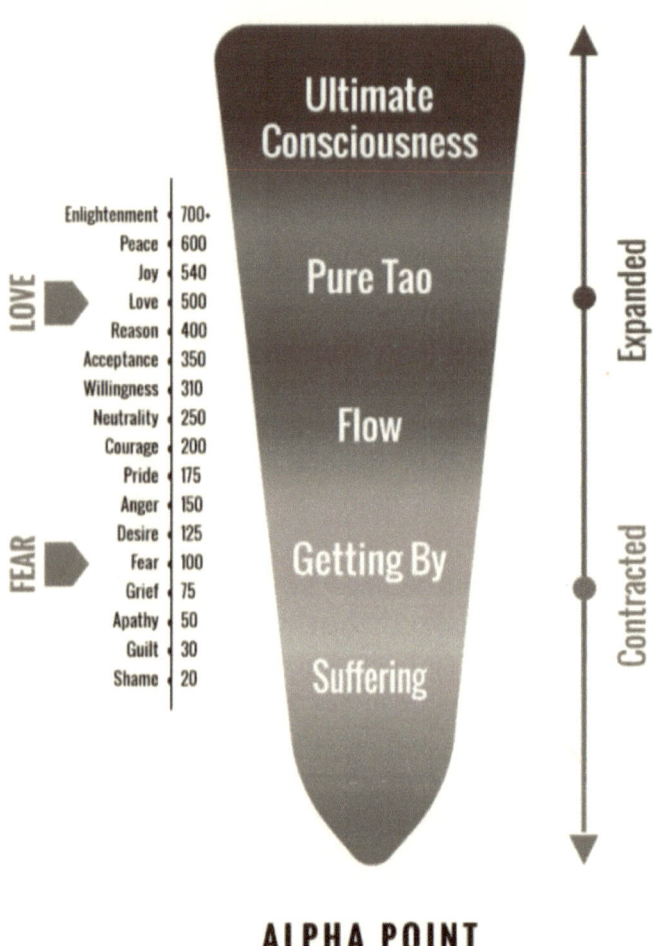

ALPHA POINT

The scale starts at the bottom at 20 and moves up to 700–1000. Think of the numbers as vibrational levels. All human beings are energetic beings that vibrate at different levels, and this scale explains what those levels are. It's important not to judge the levels as good or bad; simply see them as levels of vibrations that you have complete control over.

According to David, most human beings vibrate at around 200. The point I want to make here is that it is possible to climb the ladder of consciousness to actually reach the 700 level or above if you choose to. To do this, you must be willing to get in touch with how you feel and recognize which level you are currently on.

When I first began my spiritual journey, I was probably vibrating around 20–50. I was so filled with shame from my traumatic childhood that I had very little confidence in my ability to be loved. As I did my inner work and climbed up the ladder, I became happy and secure in all areas of my life. If I had to rate myself today based on more than 25 years of healing and transformation, I'm easily between 700 and 800. My life is filled with inner peace, joy, and purpose, and if I can get there, so can you. When I began my journey, I was definitely in hell. As a result of my own growth and healing, I now reside in heaven. This is what Jesus meant when he said, "Some of you standing here will not taste death before you enter the kingdom of heaven." I definitely experience heaven on earth regularly due to my spiritual and emotional growth.

It's important to understand that we live in a vibrational Universe and the Universe responds to our vibration. Therefore, if you are vibrating at a level 50 or so, you will attract experiences based on that same level. Anything below 100 could be considered being in a state of hell. If you are currently experiencing a lot of negative experiences in your life, rest assured you are not being punished by God; you are simply attracting experiences based on your vibration. If you want to experience more positive things in your life, you will have to increase your vibration. I'll be sharing tips on how to do this in the next chapter.

I've said this before, but I'll repeat it. The Universe is perfect by design. There is a Divine Creator, and you have a spark of divinity within you. You are completely responsible for your life and everything that shows up in it. God is love, and the only thing God can do is love you. If you do not feel loved by God, rest assured it's because you have disconnected yourself from God's love.

Commit to connecting to God's love by recognizing there is no sin and punishment or heaven and hell. There is only love, and that love is unconditional and waiting for you to access it. Jesus led the way to connecting with that love, so follow his example and you too can reside in heaven.

Here is a quote that encapsulates the message in this chapter.

Can anything ever separate us from Christ's love? Does it mean He no longer loves us if we have trouble or calamity, or are persecuted, hungry, destitute, or in danger, or threatened with death? No, despite all these things, overwhelming victory is ours through Christ, who loved us. And I am convinced that nothing can ever separate us from God's love. Neither death nor life, neither angels nor demons, neither our fears for today nor our worries about tomorrow — not even the powers of hell can separate us from God's love. No power in the sky above or in the earth below — indeed, nothing in all creation will ever be able to separate us from the love of God that is revealed in Christ Jesus our Lord. (Romans 8:35, 37-39)

"When you intentionally make the expression of LOVE a part of your daily practice- that is feeling, receiving, and giving love – not only do you boost your immune system, but you begin to understand that the more you feel love, the more you become love, and when you become love, you can change the world."

- Dr. Joe Dispenza

CHAPTER 10
Connecting To Source

I'D LIKE YOU to use your imagination and envision someone knocks at your door. When you open the door, there in the flesh stands Jesus. Initially, you're a little shocked, but you invite him in, and the two of you begin a conversation that goes something like this:

Jesus: Thanks for inviting me in. I just wanted to drop in and see how things are going for you.

You: (Still in shock) I'm doing okay, but I must admit I'm a little surprised that you're here.

Jesus: That's understandable, but don't be nervous. I'm just here to check up on you and to see if there are any questions I might be able to answer for you.

You: The truth is, I have lots of questions to ask, but I must admit, I'm a little intimidated.

Jesus: Don't be! My goal is to answer your questions and provide some insights and wisdom to support you in creating an extraordinary life. I'd like to spend the day with you and simply observe how your day goes. Are you okay with that?

You: I guess that's okay. How can I say no to Jesus?

Jesus: It's easy. Just say no. I'm not forcing you or demanding that you have to allow me to follow you. You have the choice of either saying yes or no. I'm okay either way. I won't be upset or angry no matter what you choose to do.

You: I want to say yes, but I'm feeling a little guilty because I haven't been to church in a very long time. Not only that, I've actually never read the bible. I'm feeling a little ashamed of myself for not believing you even existed.

Jesus: So let me set the record straight. I'm not here to judge you or condemn you for things you may have done in the past. I'm here to provide you with some spiritual wisdom to help you improve your life. Do not feel obligated to say yes out of fear. Choose to say yes if you're committed to improving your life.

You: Since you put it that way, I'll definitely say yes!

Jesus: That's great! This is how it will work. No one can see me or hear me except you. I will simply hang around and observe you all day, and after the day is over, we'll sit down and have a chat, and you can ask me anything you like. Sound good?

You: I'm game! Let's go!

Now imagine that Jesus follows you around the entire day. Imagine how you would act knowing he was watching you. As you're driving down the freeway and interacting with bad drivers, how would you respond? As you went to work and interacted with your coworkers, what would he see? As you spoke to your friends or partner, what would he think about how you interacted with them? What would he think about the programs you watched on TV or the music you listened to?

Now imagine in this hypothetical situation, it's the end of the day, and you're back at home, and you and Jesus are sitting on the couch continuing your conversation.

Jesus: Well, how was your day?

You: Are you kidding me? I was a nervous wreck the entire day!

Jesus: But why?

You: Because you're Jesus, that's why?

Jesus: But what has that got to do with anything?

You: Are you serious? Don't you think hanging around God all day should make me nervous?

Jesus: But I'm not God!

You: What? What a minute! What do you mean you're not God?

Jesus: Exactly what I said. I'm not God. I'm the son of God.

You: What's the difference?

Jesus: There is a big difference. God is the creator, and as I stated several times in the bible, the creator is my Father. God is the source of all things, not me.

You: But my grandmother always quoted John 10:30 from the bible which says, "I and my father are one." Doesn't that mean you are God?

Jesus: Most religions misinterpret that passage. What I meant by that was, I have a divine spark of my Father within me and we are not separate from each other. The truth is, every human being has that same spark of my Father within them. That is why I said, "These things and even greater things you shall do also." But I never said I was the source. I always gave credit to my Father, who is the true source of all things.

You: So why do most Christian religions worship and pray to you? Ever since I was a child, I was told to pray to you and that you answered prayers. Was I taught wrong?

Jesus: I wouldn't call it wrong. I would call it an error. It is an erroneous teaching that has been passed down for generations, and very few people are willing to acknowledge this truth. There is nothing wrong with praying to me and using me as a conduit for my Father's work, but ultimately you must understand I am simply the personification of the Christ energy my Father released when the Universe was created. I am not the source, my Father is. I specifically said, "I did not come to be served, but to serve." In other words, I came to serve my Father because he is the source of all of creation.

You: Well, that definitely answers one of the questions I was going to ask. Thank you for that clarification.

Jesus: Before you ask your next question, I'd like to ask you one.

You: Go right ahead.

Jesus: During the day, as I followed you around, you appeared to be a little apprehensive. Even some of your coworkers wondered what was different about you. Did you do anything differently because I was with you?

You: Of course, I did!

Jesus: But why? Why would you do things differently because I was there?

You: You've got to be kidding me! Why wouldn't I do things differently while the son of God is watching over me?

Jesus: So what did I do that made you change how you acted?

You: You didn't have to do anything. The fact that you were there is what caused me to act differently. The truth is, I've always been afraid of you. I've been afraid that you would reject me and call me a sinner for all of the mistakes I've made in my life.

Jesus: Once again, this is an issue with organized religion. Religion has spread a lot of misinformation about my Father and me. My Father and I are not to be feared but to be accepted and loved. We never judge, condemn, or punish anyone; we can only love. My purpose was to teach you how to love God, love yourself, and love others.

You: But if God only wanted to teach us how to love, why did he create the devil and evil?

Jesus: Rest assured, God did not create evil or the devil. Please accept this truth; there is but one presence and one power in the Universe, God the good, omnipotent. Man created everything else. This fictitious being you refer to as the devil was created by man through organized religion. Think about this deeply, why would a loving God create an opposing force that it would have to fight against? If God is the Creator of all things, how could God's creation even compete with the power of God? If you think deeply about this, you should conclude that it doesn't make any sense.

You: Okay, if God didn't create evil or the devil, why is your Father so angry at humanity?

Jesus: I'm not sure what you mean?

You: In the Old Testament, there are several stories in which your Father appears to be very angry. In one story, he tells a parent to kill their child if the child misbehaves. In the story of Moses, he kills the first-born son of every family, he sends a plague, he rains down fire, and he keeps his people lost in a desert for 40 years. In modern times, he sends hurricanes and earthquakes, he lets millions of people starve every day, and some of his Christian followers promote hate and violence. He sure seems like an angry God to me!

Jesus: This is one of the many problems of organized religions. They have promoted this idea that my Father is an angry, judgmental God. Nothing could be further from the truth. My Father is love. My Father is the intelligence that causes the planets to stay aligned and the human body to heal. My Father is the Source of all of creation. The bible isn't really what my Father said. The bible is man's interpretation of what they believe my Father said. The bible is a revelation inspired by my Father to help humanity understand there was a Divine Creator that created this Universe. It is a series of stories, metaphors, and allegories that share eternal truths of how God operates. Even using the metaphor that God is the Father is inaccurate in some ways because it implies that God is a human being. Because of the patriarchal makeup of the world, men use the term Father to describe God, yet it is probably more accurate to use the term Mother because it is mothers who actually give birth. God gave birth to the Universe, and men began referring to it as Father. It is actually more accurate to refer to the Creator as simply Pure Love. Pure love is the animating force of life that drives everything in the Universe. Therefore, God is definitely not angry at humanity. God is simply attempting to guide humanity back to oneness with him/it.

You: That is such a relief to hear. I've always believed in the old white guy sitting in the clouds metaphor about God, but your explanation definitely makes more sense to me and changes my perception of God.

Jesus: That was the whole intention of my showing up on this planet in the first place. God wanted to show up in physical form so that human beings would know there was a Creator and that the Creator loved its creations. My entire message was about sharing the unconditional love of God, but unfortunately, there has been a lot of misinterpretations through the different world religions.

You: With that being said, I'd really like to know what is the one true religion and who are God's chosen people.

Jesus: All people are God's chosen people, and the only true religion is love. Human beings have constructed this illusion that some human beings are better than others, which simply isn't true. God has sent several different messengers to spread the message of love, and each one actually shared the same message. Religions have distorted the primary message for decades, but ultimately every religion at its core teaches that God is love, and every human being has access to that love.

You: So, are you saying Christianity isn't the only way to God?

Jesus: I'm saying there are many paths to God, and all paths originate from the same source and lead to the same place. Did you know that I'm not a Christian? Christianity was born from my teachings, but I would not wear a label called Christian. I came to teach people how to access the Christ within themselves, not to wear a label called Christian. Christianity is the process my followers must go through if they want to embody my teachings and create their own connection to God. I came to lead by example, and anyone who follows me can gain direct access to the Christ within them.

People who may choose to follow me, Buddha, Muhammad, Krishna, or a host of other spiritual teachers, can all gain access to God if they follow our examples and focus their attention on love. It's all about love because love is the animating force of life, and it is literally God.

You: All I can say is wow! You have completely shifted everything I've believed about God. I'm no longer afraid of God, and I now commit myself to creating intimacy and connection to God that allows me to feel the love of God and to express that love to everyone I meet.

Jesus: Well, that means my work here is complete. You have opened your mind and heart to God, which tells me you are ready to embody the Christ within you. As you continue to deepen your relationship with God, know that I am just a thought and a prayer away, so do not hesitate to call on me when and if you need me. I am with you always, in all ways. All you have to do is reach out to me, and I'll be there.

You: Words cannot express how I feel right now. At the very core of my being, I feel the love of God. I want to follow in your footsteps and share that love with others. Thank you from the bottom of my heart for coming into my life and sharing your love and wisdom with me.

Jesus: Thank you for accepting my love and for becoming a vessel to share the love of God.

Imagine what would happen if Jesus actually showed up at your door one day. How would you feel? How would you act? If he followed you around for one full day, would you change how you interacted with others? There are a lot of people who claim to be Christian, and yet when you look at their life and their actions, they are definitely not consistent with the teachings of Jesus. If you go back to the chapter about What Is Christianity, it explains how Christianity is the process of becoming Christlike. When we truly become Christlike, we embody and demonstrate the true love of God just like Jesus did. We will not need a label called Christian because our actions will speak louder than the label. This should be our ultimate goal, to become Christlike and to share the love of God.

Another way to think about this is learning how to connect to the Source. God is the source of all things, and when we develop intimacy and connection to this Source, nothing is impossible. When we connect to this Source, we become a divine expression of it, and we exhibit all of the same qualities, characteristics, and attributes of it.

You may be wondering how you can connect to the Source, so I'd like to share some things which have allowed me to do so.

First of all, I believe it is imperative for you to follow Jesus' advice by seeking the kingdom within. This means you must be willing to do your inner work of healing your heart from any past trauma and getting in touch with your emotions. Remember this quote, "If you don't go within, you will always go without." In order to connect to God, you must be connected to your feelings because your feelings are the language of your Soul, and it is how God communicates with us.

Next, it's important to embrace the idea that God is the Divine Energy and Intelligence that created and is still creating this amazing Universe we live in. God is not some grey-haired bearded old guy in the clouds taking notes of your life waiting for you to sin. Since God is energy, you must connect to it energetically. Do you remember the quote from Einstein that said everything is energy? This is a literal statement. Everything is energy; therefore, so is God.

To connect to this energy, it's important to understand there are two common denominators in every major religion. It does not matter what part of the world that religion originated from; these two things will be found within that religion. Those two things are meditation and prayer.

You can follow Jesus, Buddha, Muhammad, Krishna, or any other spiritual teacher, and I can assure you that each of them taught the importance of meditation and prayer.

Since meditation is central to all religions, why is it so few people actually practice it? I believe there are a few reasons for this. One reason is people have the wrong idea of what meditation is. Most people believe meditation involves getting your mind to go blank, so you actually stop thinking. This is incorrect. Meditation isn't about making your mind go blank, it is simply the process of paying attention to what's going through your mind. Here is another way to think about it. Check out this article by scientist and meditation expert Arial Garten. (www.choosemuse.com)

Meditation is a practice, or training, that leads to healthy and positive mindsets. Mindfulness is a skill that is built as a result." In short, meditation is doing the workout, mindfulness is the result.

Meditation builds the skill of mindfulness," Ariel explains.

Mindfulness is a state of being. It means being present in the moment and having non-judgmental awareness of your thoughts, feelings, body, and environment.

While you're meditating, you place your focus on your breath, but your mind can begin to wander. Meditation teaches you to notice your mind wandering, and bring it back to focus on the task at hand.

The skill of mindfulness can be applied in a million little ways throughout our lives. When our mind wanders during a conversation, or while working, or traveling, mindfulness teaches us to make choices about where our thoughts go and bring them back to the present moment.

"Mindfulness makes the world feel alive and makes your world feel great!"

The training of meditation teaches the skill of being aware of where your thoughts are and making an intentional choice to be in the moment. Awareness and mindfulness are really the same things–you're using that skill to be aware of your thoughts and make a choice on where to focus your attention.

A study published in the journal Science found that: "46.9% of the time our minds are wandering," Ariel says, "and people who have wandering minds tend to be unhappy." Humans are unique among animals because we spend the majority of our time thinking about things that aren't right in front of us. The study found that how often our minds wander and where they go has a big impact on our happiness.

If meditation teaches us the skill of mindfulness, mindfulness helps us be happier by keeping our mind from wandering and focused on the present. This has positive impacts on your body, your relationships, and multiple aspects of your life!

The practice of meditation allows us to become aware of the thoughts flowing through our minds, and mindfulness allows us to change those thoughts if we choose to. It is not possible for your mind to go completely blank during meditation. There will always be thoughts that flow through your mind. You always have the power to change your thoughts, so developing a meditation practice gives you the tools to change them.

Here is a quote I put together that should help you grasp the benefit of meditation. "When you learn to quiet the noise of your mind and move into the silence of your heart, then you will hear the voice of your Soul." A meditation practice can help you quiet the noise of your mind so you can hear your own Soul. Your Soul is your connection to Divine Intelligence, and when you learn to listen to it, it becomes that still small voice of God that can guide you to your ultimate destiny. This is how you connect to the Source.

Meditation practice has lots of benefits. For me, what I enjoy the most is the peace of mind that comes from meditating. There was a time in my life when my mind would race so much with thinking that I would get these massive "thinking headaches" that were absolutely debilitating. They felt like migraines but were more intense. I remember one time when my mind was racing so fast that I wrote in my journal that I wished I could turn my mind off. I just wanted my mind to shut off so I could be at peace. These headaches prompted me to begin a meditation practice in an attempt to alleviate them. As a result of my meditation practice, I have not had a "thinking headache" in more than 20 years.

Without question, inner peace is one of the greatest benefits of meditation.

Another benefit of meditation is creativity. Before I began my meditation practice, I had no idea what creativity was. After learning to meditate, I discovered that I have several unique gifts and talents, and one of those talents is writing. I never dreamed of being a writer. As a matter of fact, I didn't start writing until after going to therapy in my thirties when I started writing in a journal. Since learning to meditate, I have written ten books, hosted four different podcasts, produced and hosted a cable TV show, and currently have three TV channels on the Roku network. I know beyond a shadow of a doubt all of this is a result of learning to meditate. Meditation opened the floodgates of creativity, and I am absolutely convinced that I would have never accomplished the things I've done without meditation.

But for me, the greatest benefit of meditation is developing intimacy and connection to Divine Intelligence. It's been said that "knowing is the complete absence of doubt," and I know with every fiber of my being that Divine Intelligence is real, and I have direct access and connection to it. It is a feeling and a "knowingness" that this intelligence is in me, and it is what connects me to all things. It is this connection that brings me joy beyond description and immeasurable faith and trust.

If you're truly committed to connecting to the Source, it is imperative that you begin a meditation practice. I am not aware of any other practice that allows you to connect and experience Divine Intelligence. It is no accident that every single religion or spiritual practice includes some form of meditation, so rest assured it is a trusted and tested method of connecting with the divine.

Starting a meditation practice can be confusing and somewhat difficult at first, but it is up to you to find a practice that you are comfortable with and committed to and then incorporate it into your life.

There is a part of you that will resist this and talk you out of trying it, but you must not listen to that part of yourself. I remember the very first time I attempted to meditate; my mind went into overdrive, trying to talk me out of it. As a matter of fact, I remember the very first thoughts that went through my mind the first time I tried it. "This is stupid! What are you doing? You're becoming one of those new-age guys. You don't have time for this." These were the exact words that went through my mind. I remember it because I actually wrote them down in my journal.

Remember what I said about the Big S Self and the Little S Self? Your Little S Self is that part of you that will try and convince you not to do this. Its job is to keep you safe and comfortable, and trying new things will definitely make it uncomfortable. Your job is not to pay attention to your Little S Self. Your job is to listen to your Big S Self, which is the part of you that caused you to read this book, and it is the part of you that wants you to grow and connect to Divine Intelligence.

Learn to listen to and trust that part of you because it is the part that will guide you to find the right meditation practice. So begin by doing a little research. There is an infinite amount of resources online for meditation. Here are a couple that I highly recommend. www.craighamiltonglobal.net, www.drjoedispenza.com and www.chopra-centermeditation.com The key is to find a teacher and a practice you feel comfortable with and commit to your practice. Understand there is no "wrong way" to do meditation. You simply have to commit to the practice and be consistent with it.

Another important part of connecting with Source is prayer. Like meditation, prayer is a part of every single religion on the planet. It has been around since the beginning of time, and it is how we communicate with Divine Intelligence. Simply stated, prayer means talking to God. It does not necessarily mean begging so God will answer your prayers; it means creating an open line of communication between you and Divine Intelligence.

When you think about prayer, you may be inclined to think about it from a religious perspective. I invite you not to do that, but instead, I'd like you to see it through the lens of science. Remember when I said everything is energy? If this is true, that means thoughts are energy also. Since we live in an energetic vibrational Universe, this means whatever we think about, we bring about. This is why the law of attraction works. Whether you realize it or not, in some ways, you are always praying because you are always thinking, and thoughts are energy and the Universe responds to that energy.

Now ask yourself this question: If you knew every thought you had was creative, would you still think the same thoughts you are thinking on a regular basis?

The truth of the matter is it's true. Whether you're conscious of it or not, every thought you have is actually creative. As you look at your life, you should be able to see what your primary thoughts are. If your life is filled with joy and abundance, rest assured it is the result of most of your thoughts.

On the other hand, if your life is filled with anger and scarcity, I can assure you it is a reflection of the majority of things you think about. This is why it's been said, "As a man thinketh in his heart so shall he be."

So, what are you thinking about?

When we learn to focus our attention on what we think, we are actually engaged in prayer. Prayer is simply concentrated thought, so it is imperative that you ask yourself what you are thinking about on a regular basis.

There is currently a large body of scientific evidence that proves how prayer works. A really good book that breaks prayer down through quantum physics is Healing Words by Dr. Larry Dossey. It is a fascinating book that breaks down the science behind prayer and how and why prayer works. I highly recommend you read it.

I'd like to share an experience I had with prayer that literally changed my life. After being an Atheist for a few years, I started to believe in a power greater than myself. It was extremely difficult at first, but as I learned to combine science with spirituality, my mind and heart became open to the possibility of God being real. One Sunday at Unity church, the minister had a sermon about the power of prayer, and she mentioned how she used songs as prayers. She invited the congregation to choose one of their favorite songs and use it as a prayer and apply it to a current challenge they may have been dealing with.

For me, the challenge was to have an experience of God that would confirm for me that God was real. I had been praying for God to give me a sign, an irrefutable sign that it was real. In other words, I wanted proof that God existed. So I took her advice and chose one of my favorite songs titled I Want To Know What Love Is by the group Foreigner. It was absolutely perfect because the chorus line says:

I wanna know what love is
I want you to show me
I wanna feel what love is
I know you can show me"

These words reflected exactly what I was feeling and what I wanted to say to God. My prayer was to feel the love of God, and I wanted God to show me how to do that. So this song became my prayer and mantra, and I would listen to it at least twice a day during my morning and evening meditations.

After a few weeks, I was sitting out in nature by a lake while listening to the song on my music player with headphones. It was a beautiful sunny day, and I was in one of my favorite places to meditate. As I listened to the song and looked at all of the beauty that surrounded me, all of a sudden, I felt this incredible warmth in my chest. As I continued to admire the beauty, I remembered the amazing journey I had been on for the past several years, and I realized in that very moment I was probably happier than I'd ever felt in my life. As a result of the amazing transformational journey I had been on, I felt a deep sense of inner peace and serenity that I hadn't felt before, even though I was financially broke with very few material possessions. Suddenly, I was overcome with gratitude, and I began thanking God for carrying me through some extremely difficult times. I then remembered this beautiful poem called, Footsteps In The Sand by Mary Stevenson:

One night I dreamed a dream.
As I was walking along the beach with my Lord.
Across the dark sky flashed scenes from my life.
For each scene, I noticed two sets of footprints in the sand,
One belonging to me and one to my Lord.

After the last scene of my life flashed before me,
I looked back at the footprints in the sand.
I noticed that at many times along the path of my life,
Especially at the very lowest and saddest times,
There was only one set of footprints.

This really troubled me, so I asked the Lord about it.
"Lord, you said once I decided to follow you,
You'd walk with me all the way.
But I noticed that during the saddest and most troublesome times of my life,

Chapter 10: Connecting To Source

There was only one set of footprints.
I don't understand why, when I needed You the most, You would leave me."

He whispered, "My precious child, I love you and will never leave you
Never, ever, during your trials and adversities.
When you saw only one set of footprints,
It was then that I carried you."

As I thought about that poem, I realized that God had been with me always, and during the most difficult times (and there were many), it was when God was carrying me. Even when I didn't believe in God, God was right there carrying me through all of the adversities I had experienced.

Suddenly, it felt as if my heart burst open with gratitude, and I felt this amazing rush of energy that moved through my body. It was a physical sensation that caused my entire body to become warm to the touch. It was so intense that my body was literally shaking. I then began to cry tears of joy, realizing that God had given me exactly what I had prayed for at that moment. I was experiencing the love of God, and it was the proof I needed to know that God was real.

Words could never come close to explaining the feeling of love I felt at that moment. It was a love so deep that I will never be able to deny the existence of God again. It was a love that came from the deepest recesses of my heart, and it confirmed my connection to Divine Intelligence.

This experience was made possible because of my commitment to meditation and prayer, and if I can have that experience, I know you can also. Through meditation and prayer, I was able to connect to the Source of all things, and it has allowed me to create a connection that can never be broken, and I hope that you have the opportunity to experience it for yourself.

My intention with this book was to share the lessons I've learned from the past twenty-five years of my own spiritual journey to support you in your spiritual journey. In summary, I hope this book has provided you with some insights and wisdom that lets you know first and foremost that God is real, and it is up to you to connect with God in whatever way feels right for you. You must embrace the fact that God is love, and you're an expression of that love. If you are experiencing any type of pain or discomfort, remember it simply means you have disconnected from the love which God is, and it is your responsibility to reconnect to Divine Intelligence. You have never been, nor will you ever be punished by God. God can only do one thing, and that one thing is love. God loves you, and you are lovable and worthy of that love. The simplest way to know if you're connected to God is by checking in with how you feel. Do you feel loved, accepted, joyful, nurtured, grateful, optimistic, compassionate, caring, forgiving, and self-confident? If the answer is yes, then you are connected to God. If the answer is no, it's up to you to get reconnected.

Never forget that Jesus was your brother and your way-shower, and he came to teach you how to enter the kingdom of heaven and connect to his Father, which is Divine Intelligence. He did not come to be served but to serve his Father, and that is what he expects of you.

So, remember his most important commandment. "Love the Lord your God with all of your heart, and with all of your soul, and with all of your mind. And the second is like it, Love your neighbor as yourself."

So to answer the question I posed in the title of this book, "What If Jesus Were A Coach," my answer would be, if Jesus were a coach, he would teach you how to connect to Divine Intelligence and gain access to his Father so that you could create the life of your dreams. That was his ultimate purpose and destiny, and I believe he fulfilled it beautifully.

I'll close this book with two of my all-time favorite prayers that helped me connect to God and know beyond a shadow of a doubt that God is real. These two prayers are songs that express my deepest thoughts and feelings about God. The first one is I Want To Know What Love Is, by Foreigner. It was the song that opened my heart to

God and allowed me to feel the presence of God. The second one is, Because You Loved Me by Celine Dion. It is a song and prayer that I sing to God on a regular basis as a way of expressing my deeply felt gratitude for my connection to God. The words express exactly what I would say to Jesus if he showed up on my doorstep one day.

My request is that you listen to these songs, and as you read them, allow yourself to feel the depth of the words and messages contained within them.

Good luck and stay blessed, because you are!

Take care,

Michael

**I Want to Know What Love Is
by Foreigner**

[Verse 1]

I've gotta take a little time
A little time to think things over
I better read between the lines
In case I need it when I'm older

This mountain, I must climb
Feels like a world upon my shoulders
Through the clouds, I see love shine
Keeps me warm as life grows colder

In my life, there's been heartache and pain
I don't know if I can face it again
Can't stop now, I've traveled so far
To change this lonely life

[Chorus]

I wanna know what love is
I want you to show me
I wanna feel what love is
I know you can show me (hey)

[Verse2]
Gotta take a little time
Little time to look around me
I've got nowhere left to hide
Looks like love has finally found me

In my life, there's been heartache and pain
I don't know if I can face it again
Can't stop now, I've traveled so far
To change this lonely life

[Chorus]

I wanna know what love is
I want you to show me
I wanna feel what love is
I know you can show me

I wanna know what love is (I wanna know)
I want you to show me (I wanna feel)
I wanna feel what love is (I know, I know, and I know)
I know you can show me
Let's talk about love

I wanna know what love is
(Love that you feel inside)
I want you to show me
(I'm feeling so much love)
I wanna feel what love is
(And you know, you just can't hide)
I know you can show me

Oh, I wanna know what love is
(Let's talk about love)
I know you can show me
(I wanna feel)
I wanna feel what love is
(And you know you just can't hide)

I know you can show me
I wanna feel what love is (oh, I wanna know)
I want you to show me

**Because You Loved Me
by Celine Dion**

[Verse 1]

For all those times you stood by me
For all the truth that you made me see
For all the joy you brought to my life
For all the wrong that you made right
For every dream you made come true
For all the love I found in you
I would be forever thankful, baby
You're the one who held me up
Never let me fall
You're the one who saw me through, through it all

[Chorus]

You were my strength when I was weak
You were my voice when I couldn't speak
You were my eyes when I couldn't see
You saw the best there was in me
Lifted me up when I couldn't reach
You gave me faith 'cause you believed
I'm everything I am
Because you loved me

[Verse 2]

You gave me wings and made me fly
You touched my hand, I could touch the sky
I lost my faith, you gave it back to me
You said no star was out of reach
You stood by me and I stood tall

I had your love, I had it all
I'm grateful for each day you gave me
Maybe I don't know that much
But I know this much is true
I was blessed because I was loved by you

[Chorus]

You were my strength when I was weak (You were my strength)
You were my voice when I couldn't speak
You were my eyes when I couldn't see
You saw the best there was in me
Lifted me up when I couldn't reach
You gave me faith 'cause you believed
I'm everything I am
Because you loved me

[Verse 3]

You were always there for me
The tender wind that carried me
A light in the dark, shining your love into my life
You've been my inspiration
Through the lies, you were the truth
My world is a better place because of you

[Chorus]

You were my strength when I was weak (You were my strength)
You were my voice when I couldn't speak (When I couldn't speak)
You were my eyes when I couldn't see
You saw the best there was in me
Lifted me up when I couldn't reach
You gave me faith 'cause you believed
I'm everything I am
Because you loved me
You were my strength when I was weak
You were my voice when I couldn't speak (My voice)
You were my eyes when I couldn't see
You saw the best there was in me

Lifted me up when I couldn't reach
You gave me faith 'cause you believed
I'm everything I am
Because you loved me
Oh

[Outro]

I'm everything I am
Because you loved me

Bio

Coach Michael Taylor is an entrepreneur, author (10 books), motivational speaker, podcaster, and radio and TV show host who has dedicated his life to empowering men and women to reach their full potential by transforming their lives from the inside out. He knows first-hand how to overcome adversity and build a rewarding and fulfilling life and he is sharing his knowledge and wisdom with others to support them in creating the life of their dreams. www.coachmichaeltaylor.com

He was featured in the bestselling book Motivational Speakers America with speaking legends Les Brown and Brian Tracey, and he is also an Amazon.com bestselling author. He has won numerous awards for his dynamic speaking style and he has been featured on multiple radio and TV interviews across the country.

He is President & CEO of Creation Publishing Group which is a company that specializes in creating programs and products that empower men and women to create extraordinary lives and he currently hosts three television channels on the Roku Television Network.

Most importantly he has been blissfully married for 19 years to the woman of his dreams and he is a proud father to three grown children whom he is extremely proud of.

When he isn't writing or speaking you'll find him checking out the latest movies or listening to old school 70's and 80's soul music and contemporary jazz.

He considers himself to be an irrepressible optimist with a passion for the impossible and he believes there has never been a better time to be alive on this planet than right now.

Resources

Recommended reading:

Conversations With God by Neale Donald Walsch
The Seat Of The Soul by Gary Zukav
A Return To Love By Marianne Williamson
The Spontaneous Fulfillment of Desire by Deepak Chopra
The Code Of The Extraordinary Mind by Vishen Lakhiani
Power Versus Force by David Hawkins
Think And Grow Rich by Napoleon Hill
You Are The Placebo by Dr. Joe Dispenza

Recommended sites:

www.unity.org
www.mindvalley.com
www.agapelive.com
www.tut.com
www.drjoedispenza.com

Coach Michael Taylor podcasts:

Don't Believe The Hype - https://anchor.fm/dontbelievethehype
Shatter The Stereotypes - https://anchor.fm/shatterthestereotypes
A New Conversation With Men - https://anchor.fm/ancwm
Joy Passion & Profit - https://anchor.fm/joypassionprofit

Coach Michael Taylor YouTube Channels

Shatter The Stereotypes
Coach Michael Taylor
Joy Passion Profit

www.ingramcontent.com/pod-product-compliance
Lightning Source LLC
Chambersburg PA
CBHW030908080526
44589CB00010B/198